Buddha Vajradhara

The Supreme Siddhi of Mahamudra

Teachings, Poems, and Songs of the
Drukpa Kagyu Lineage

SELECTED TRANSLATIONS BY

Gerardo Abboud
Adam Kane
Sean Price

WITH AN INTRODUCTION BY

Tsoknyi Rinpoche

SNOW LION
BOULDER
2017

Snow Lion
An imprint of Shambhala Publications, Inc.
4720 Walnut Street
Boulder, Colorado 80301
www.shambhala.com

9 8 7 6 5 4 3 2 1

First Edition
Printed in the United States of America

⊛ This edition is printed on acid-free paper that meets the American
National Standards Institute Z39.48 Standard.
♻ Shambhala makes every effort to print on recycled paper.
For more information please visit www.shambhala.com.

Distributed in the United States by Penguin Random House LLC
and in Canada by Random House of Canada Ltd

LIBRARY OF CONGRESS CATALOGING-IN-PUBLICATION DATA

Names: Abboud, Gerardo, translator. | Kane, Adam, 1978– translator. | Price, Sean, 1968–
translator. | Tsoknyi Rinpoche, writer of introduction.
Title: The supreme siddhi of Mahamudra: teachings, poems, and songs of the Drukpa Kagyu
lineage / selected translations by Gerardo Abboud, Adam Kane, and Sean Price; foreword by
Tsoknyi Rinpoche.
Description: First edition. | Boulder: Snow Lion, 2017. | Includes bibliographical references.
Identifiers: LCCN 2017009904 | ISBN 9781559394680 (hardback)
Subjects: LCSH: 'Brug-pa (Sect) | BISAC: RELIGION / Buddhism / Sacred Writings. |
RELIGION / Buddhism / History. | RELIGION / Buddhism / Tibetan.
Classification: LCC BQ7683 .S87 2017 | DDC 294.3/923—dc23
LC record available at https://lccn.loc.gov/2017009904

This collection is dedicated with a deep sense of love and gratitude to the late Drubwang Dorzong Rinpoche and to Juani Loizaga de Abboud.

Contents

FOREWORD

This book is an extraordinary collection of spiritual treasures. It includes enlightened poems, *dohas*, ancient writings, and practical instructions of the profound essential practices of Mahamudra composed by the great Kagyu forefathers and some of the most eminent masters of the Drukpa Kagyu lineage from the eleventh to twentieth century.

I am delighted that this long-awaited English translation has finally been published. I would like to extend my deepest appreciation to everyone who helped to make this book possible. Particular thanks to Sean Price, Gerardo Abboud, and Adam Kane, learned and devoted translators whose unwavering dedication and hard work gave birth to an unprecedented English version of the Drukpa Kagyu teachings.

This book is a condensed elixir of the enlightened minds and an indispensable treasure to anyone who is pursuing the ultimate aim of liberation. May it instill great inspiration and confidence in the fortunate ones and open wide the doors of pure virtue and goodness. Through seeking clarification and following the oral advice of a qualified guru, vast benefit is certain to ensue from reading this collection.

We dedicate this book to the unsurpassable happiness and enlightenment of all mother-beings.

Drukpa Chögon Rinpoche
July 10, 2016

Translators' Introduction

Not all those with squinting warm-looking eyes are called
    bodhisattvas . . .
To spout hundreds of words is not what is meant by
    explanation . . .
To translate colloquial language into Tibetan is not what is called
    a translation . . .

        —From *The Song of Not All* by Drukpa Kunleg

This collection of translations captures a rich cross section of Mahamudra, the practice of the sublime essential nature, from the Drukpa Kagyu lineage of Tibetan Buddhism. The Drukpa branch of Kagyu is perhaps best known for its yogic masters living in remote mountain retreats and its wandering enlightened madmen. They often taught in direct and piercing ways—spontaneously expressing their love, devotion, and liberating insight. The Drukpa tradition also excelled at meticulous systematized expressions of the Mahamudra path.

    Spanning from the Bengali mahasiddha Tilopa in the tenth century through generations of renowned Tibetan masters such as Marpa, Milarepa, Tsangpa Gyare, Drukpa Kunleg, and Pema Karpo, all the way to the contemporary masters Togden Shakya Shri, the Eighth Khamtrul Rinpoche, and Adeu Rinpoche, these texts provide a sample of over one thousand years of transmission. The translations in this volume are arranged in chronological order to give a sense of the historical progression. There are visions, poems, songs, heartfelt instructions, detailed meditation manuals and even a meaty philosophical defense of the four yogas of Mahamudra. For any Buddhist or other spiritual practitioner wishing to dive into the rich tradition of Mahamudra, this will be a sublime feast.

THE MAHAMUDRA TRADITION

As Tsoknyi Rinpoche's introduction addresses the lineage and practices of the Drukpa Kagyu, here we will discuss how Mahamudra relates to sutric and tantric Buddhism, briefly explore the origin of essence Mahamudra instructions, and share how this project unfolded. The Drukpa Kagyu tradition is one of the most widespread and distinguished in Tibetan Buddhism, illustrated by a famous Tibetan saying: "Half of Tibetans are Drukpas; half of Drukpas are wandering yogins; and half of wandering yogins are realized." The spread of Drukpa even spilled over the borders of Tibet, contributing to the creation of Dharma kingdoms in Bhutan (whose name "Druk" comes from the Drukpa lineage), Ladakh, and Mustang.

Many thousands of great Drukpa lamas have appeared over the past eight hundred years as well as countless disciples. The Drukpa Kagyu lineage includes brilliant scholars, such as Pema Karpo, crazy wisdom masters, such as Drukpa Kunleg, revered yogis, such as Lingchen Repa and Götsangpa, and these lamas have made a huge footprint of compassionate action. Despite its sizable impact in the Tibetan Buddhist world, the Drukpa Kagyu lineage is relatively unknown in the West where only a handful of books have been published and relatively few Dharma centers have been established. We hope this collection will spark more appreciation of the Drukpa Kagyu teachings.

The Drukpa, like other Kagyu traditions, emphasizes the direct experience of meditation practice. With a foundation of deep devotion and a lifestyle guided by renunciation, the essential motivation for Drukpa practitioners is *bodhichitta*—the wish to attain awakening in order to free all beings from suffering. From the full spectrum of teachings contained in the Drukpa tradition, we have focused this collection on Mahamudra songs and meditation manuals, as these are the Drukpa's most celebrated contributions. As the Sanskrit term "mahamudra" made its way into Tibetan (and now into English), it has been translated and explained in many ways. A direct translation of "mahamudra" is "The Great Seal," which is often explained as the single "seal" of reality or the nature of all phenomena. Depending on the teacher and context, this single nature is equated with emptiness, great bliss, or with the "natural state of mind." The Tibetan word for *mahamudra* (*chakgya chenpo*) is a four-syllable rendering: *chak* + *gya* (meaning "seal") and *chen* + *po* (meaning "great"). Being a seminal term, each of the four major schools of Tibetan Buddhism has unpacked the term in various ways. Götsangpa Gonpo Dorje (1189–1258), an early Drukpa master, offered an explanation from the *Mahamudratilaka Tantra*:

> As for its etymology, it is said, "*Chak* refers to the original wisdom of emptiness, *gya* refers to freedom from samsaric experience, and *chen po* refers to the realization of their unity."[1]

Tibetan Buddhism is unique in that it contains and upholds all the major approaches (also known as vehicles) of Indian Buddhism, spanning the Shravakayana and Mahayana teachings of the Sutra systems, and the Vajrayana teachings of the tantric systems. Both sutric and tantric streams of Indian Buddhism indeed entered Tibet during the early (*ngadar*) and later (*chidar*) waves of transmission. In the context of receiving these differing approaches to the path, each lineage in each school needed a central organizing principle to clarify their particular system of integrating the views of Sutra and Tantra. For the Kagyu traditions, including the Drukpa Kagyu, that organizing principle is Mahamudra—the underlying thread that explains how the whole basis, path, and fruition works, whether on the causal level of Sutra or the resultant level of Tantra. The reason that Mahamudra serves as this crux is that it directly addresses buddha-nature and emptiness, how they can be actualized.

The buddha-nature (*tathagatagarba*) principle is a profound topic, which is beyond the scope of this present discussion. Here it is sufficient to mention that buddha-nature is often described as the doctrinal bridge between Sutra and Tantra. Most Kagyu schools, including the Drukpa Kagyu, explain buddha-nature as the empty and luminous nature of mind, which is full of enlightened qualities. Although temporarily veiled by our cognitive and emotional obscurations, buddha-nature always abides as the basic substance of the mind, and can be revealed as the underlying natural state by a qualified teacher. Though normally obscured, buddha-nature can be recognized in the intervals between thoughts, the seeming continuity of our conceptual and emotional patterning. Once recognized, even thoughts and emotions themselves can be experienced as expressions of buddha-nature.

This very brief introduction to Mahamudra raises two significant questions: How does Mahamudra fit into models of the path and who are these teachings for? Mahamudra was classically embedded in the tantric system of the four empowerments and the four mudras, but similar to the Great Completion (Dzogchen) teachings of the Nyingma tradition, Mahamudra can be difficult to categorize. Various masters and scholars have considered mahamudra in different ways. Some scholars describe the "three paths" of Sutra, Tantra, and essence Mahamudra, thus placing Mahamudra in a class of its own. Other scholars articulate three distinct styles of Mahamudra teaching—Sutra Mahamudra, Tantra Mahamudra, and essence Mahamudra. These different expressions primarily reflect whether sutric or tantric methods, or neither, are used as the framework within which Mahamudra practice unfolds. From an integrated perspective, Sutra, Tantra, and essence Mahamudra converge as a single tradition, with the particular skillful means being chosen by the teacher to refine the coarse and subtle dimensions of mind, depending on the karmic propensity and maturity of the student. In the end, all approaches can be seen to converge on the essence Mahamudra instructions, which directly address the subtlest aspect of mind, buddha-nature itself.[2]

Essence Mahamudra teachings are often spontaneously presented, however, and thus needed to be systematized into a clear and comprehensive overview of the path to serve as the backbone of Kagyu practice. The structure that achieved this is the four yogas of Mahamudra—one-pointedness, simplicity, one taste, and non meditation. The four-yoga model for Mahamudra is similar to a *lam rim* system (stages of the path)—providing a clear framework that describes how realization unfolds from beginning to enlightenment. Another significant role the four-yoga model plays is as a bridge between Sutra, Tantra, and essence Mahamudra. The various Kagyu schools, and even the masters within each school, have analyzed and explained the four yogas in many ways. Sometimes the first two yogas are associated with Sutra and the latter two yogas with Tantra. Sometimes the four yogas are correlated with the ten bodhisattvas *bhumis* (levels) or the five paths of Mahayana practice. In this collection, pithy and detailed teachings on the four yogas are found in *Notes on Mahamudra*, *Distinguishing the Four Yogas with Certainty*, and *Pointing Out the Sublime Essential Meaning*, all by Pema Karpo.

Containing both spontaneous pith instructions and systematized expressions, Mahamudra also serves to bridge sudden and gradual models of enlightenment. For example, it is understood that different types of individuals traverse the four yogas in various ways. The Drukpa Kagyu explains that there are three basic categories of practitioners: *instantaneous* realizers, *evanescent* types or those who leap through the path but whose experience can be unstable, and the *gradualist* step-by-step type. Based on these three types, some masters assert that there are likewise three ways of traversing the four yogas. Other masters have asserted that the four-yoga model of Mahamudra is optimally suited for the evanescent type.

As mentioned, this collection includes references to sutric, tantric, and essence Mahamudra teachings. In terms of the Sutra view, teachings on the essential recognition of emptiness within the context of Mahamudra are directly connected with the core insight of the philosophy of the Middle Way (Madhyamaka). Pema Karpo flushes out this connection in the first two sections of *Pointing Out the Sublime Essential Meaning*. Many classic Kagyu meditation manuals present Mahamudra instructions in terms of *shamatha* (calm abiding) and *vipashyana* (insight), which form the framework of Sutra Mahamudra practice. This structure can be seen in *Notes on Mahamudra* by Pema Karpo and *Opening the Door to Liberation* by Togden Shakya Shri.

In the Vajrayana tradition, *mahamudra* usually refers to the wisdom that dawns as a result of the highest stage of initiation, the seal of the unity of bliss and emptiness. References to Vajrayana frameworks and practices can be seen in many of the texts here, especially *A Vision of Saraha* by Marpa, *The Bardo Supplication* by the Second Drukchen Rinpoche, *Essence of Refined Gold* and *The Two Truths in Union* by the Third Khamtrul Rinpoche, and *Opening the Door to Liberation* and *Milarepa Supplication* by Togden Shakya Shri.

It is also significant that essence Mahamudra occupies a special position of its own due to its sole focus of direct perception. While direct perception is also a special provision of the tantric path, essence Mahamudra does not rely on the four-mudra system or indeed any of the formal tantric practices. Rather, just based on the bestowal of pointing-out instructions and the blessings of the guru (coupled with the sharp faculties of the student), emptiness can be directly experienced. Since accessing this resultant state of the empty luminous mind forms the basis of meditation training, Mahamudra is considered a resultant path, which distinguishes it from the causal Sutra paths.[3] Essence Mahamudra instructions are found throughout this collection, but especially in the *Ganges Mahamudra* by Tilopa, *Condensed Verses of Mahamudra* by Naropa, *The Single Sufficient Path of Mahamudra* by Gampopa, *Notes on*

Mahamudra by Pema Karpo, *Essence of Refined Gold* by the Third Khamtrul Rinpoche, *The Blessed Vase* by Tsele Natsok Rangdrol, and *Opening the Door to Liberation* by Togden Shakya Shri.

There is considerable debate among scholars and historians about whether the Mahamudra tradition originated in India, but there seem to be clear expressions of the spirit of the tradition in the songs and teachings of the Indian mahasiddhas, especially Saraha, Tilopa, and Maitripa. However, before Gampopa (1079–1153), Mahamudra as it is understood today was probably not a fully developed path independent from higher tantric initiations. Gampopa seems to have innovated an approach of directly introducing the view of Mahamudra to a wide spectrum of students including those uninitiated in higher tantric practices. Gampopa maintained that with either a foundation in the classic shamatha and vipashyana practices of the Sutra system, or even just by possessing strong faith and devotion for the teacher, students could successfully recognize the essential view of Mahamudra (the nature of mind) and gradually progress in sustaining and stabilizing that recognition. It is quite significant that essence Mahamudra teachings can be given to people without higher tantric initiation. This opened the door for laypeople, who often did not have the time or the philosophical and ritual background for extensive tantric practice, to receive pith instructions that express the very heart of the path. Essence Mahamudra teachings, sometimes referred to as the distilled nectar of all the Sutras and Tantras, were released from their "seal of secrecy" and made available for a much larger audience. As modern practitioners, we are fortunate beneficiaries of this approach.

In brief, by virtue of its emphasis on both emptiness and buddha-nature, Mahamudra can be viewed as a bridge between Sutra and Tantra, which can be combined with either approach. There are also essence Mahamudra instructions that are given independently of either sutric or tantric methods that involve directly pointing out the nature of the mind. In the tradition of Gampopa, whether there is prior tantric initiation or not, these instructions can be experienced by those with strong faith and devotion, and ideally with a background in shamatha and vipashyana. For genuine progress to be made on the path, a qualified teacher needs to introduce and guide a student through their experiences. For those without access to a qualified teacher, these teachings can serve to arouse faith, inspiration, and interest in these teachings, and to clarify doubts and questions. This discussion of Mahamudra is meant to provide some context for the variety of pithy and detailed Mahamudra instructions found in this collection.

THE COLLECTION OF DRUKPA KAGYU WORKS

This project was conceived several years ago by Tsoknyi Rinpoche. Aware that many Drukpa texts had not yet been translated into English, he envisioned a collection that would be practical—English translations that Dharma students could reference while receiving teachings from Drukpa Kagyu lamas. The idea for this collection gained momentum during several conversations Rinpoche had with Drukpa Chögon Rinpoche, Gerardo Abboud, Sean Price, and me, Adam Kane. It was decided that the three translators would divide up the texts and translate the collection together. It was also proposed that a scholar should draw up a list of classic Drukpa Kagyu texts. Khenpo Shedrup, a learned Bhutanese monk who resides in Swayambhu, Nepal, was asked to assist with the project. He kindly drafted a list of quintessential Drukpa texts and copied several of them from his own library. With a *karchak* (table of contents) in hand, the texts were divided up and the translators began our work. We drew on the knowledge and experience of many lamas and khenpos, consulting frequently to clarify the texts. It took roughly a year to complete the first drafts of these translations.

Most collections of this nature reflect a single translator's work. Every translator brings a unique perspective and experience to their renderings, and unavoidably our styles have their own unique flavors. We felt this would provide for a juicier collection—these Drukpa texts refracted through three lenses instead of just one. The texts were lightly edited to harmonize word choices, general formatting, and style. But as the readers will see, some unique flavors are still there. We hope you will find this range enriching.

A few of these texts, most notably the *Ganges Mahamudra* by Tilopa, are beloved classics and have been translated and published before. Why, you might ask, did we bother to do them again? Mainly because they form an integral part of the Drukpa Mahamudra lineage and they are essential to any significant collection of the tradition. Another reason is that over the millennium several versions of these texts have been transmitted, and we felt translating them in the context of Drukpa literature would be a valuable contribution.

Gerardo Abboud, from Argentina, has been studying and practicing Tibetan Buddhism, primarily in the Drukpa Kagyu tradition, for over four decades and has translated for many great lamas, including H.H. Dalai Lama, into English and Spanish. Gerardo founded and teaches at Dongyu Ling, a flourishing Dharma center in Argentina. Sean Price, a British monk from Shechen Monastery in Nepal, has been working with the Tsadra Foundation to preserve, edit, and publish Tibetan texts from all lineages of Tibetan Buddhism for many years. Adam Kane, an American, has a background in the Thai Forest Tradition of Theravada Buddhism and an MA in Buddhist Studies from the Rangjung Yeshe Institute. He studied and interpreted for several years in a *shedra* (Tibetan Buddhist study college) in Nepal. We wish to specifically thank Tsoknyi Rinpoche, Chögon Rinpoche, the late Dorzong Rinpoche, Chögyal Rinpoche, Tashi Gyaltsen Rinpoche, and Khenpo Shedrup, and all the others who kindly assisted in understanding the meaning of the texts. We also wish to thank Casey Kemp, our patient and knowledgeable editor at Shambhala Publications, who skillfully edited the manuscript and helped guide the project from a first draft to a polished book.

The translators take full responsibility and apologize for any mistakes.

May this volume be a cherished companion to all students of Mahamudra in particular and Buddhism in general. May all beings be inspired and guided by the wisdom teachings of the Drukpa Kagyu!

Adam Kane
(on behalf of the translation team)
December 2016

INTRODUCTION BY
TSOKNYI RINPOCHE

OVERVIEW OF THE LINEAGE

The Drukpa Kagyu lineage teachings come from the Tathagata Buddha Shakyamuni, who taught three major paths: the Shravakayana centers on the four noble truths, the Paramitayana expounds the meaning of emptiness, and the secret mantra teachings of the Vajrayana. The vast content of these three approaches can be condensed into the two systems of Sutra and Tantra. In terms of essential meaning, all Buddhist teachings can be summarized as addressing the two truths, the relative and ultimate. The purpose of studying, contemplating, and meditating on the two truths is to realize selflessness and emptiness. This collection is about Mahamudra, which is part of the Vajrayana approach.

In general, all Kagyu lineage teachers taught the approaches of both Sutra and Tantra. This book focuses on teachings by Drukpa Kagyu masters, who belong to a branch of the larger Kagyu tradition. The Drukpa masters practice all three vehicles of the Buddha's teachings. The lamas first studied and trained in the Sutra system, and then learned and practiced the tantric systems all the way up to the pinnacle, the essence of Tantra, which is called Mahamudra. By practicing the view, meditation, and conduct of Mahamudra, direct realization was born in their minds. All the lamas of this lineage practiced in this way.

These masters often expressed their realization in the form of poetic songs, called *dohas* or *vajra* songs. These songs do not follow the style of extensive commentary on major philosophical treatises.

Rather, the yogins expressed the very essence of the practice in spontaneous and experiential ways. Along with detailed guidance manuals, advice for retreat, and various pith instructions, this collection contains a selection of vajra songs from among the great many masters that we have in the lineage.

THE LINEAGE MASTERS

As for the origin of these teachings, the human source was the mahasiddha Tilopa. Tilopa's special lineage was called "The Four Oral Transmissions of the Siddhas." The *dharmakaya* Buddha Vajradhara entrusted these four lineages to the bodhisattva Vajrapani, the Lord of Secrets, who passed them to four accomplished masters, called siddhas. These four siddhas passed on their oral lineages, as well as their blessings, to Tilopa. The four oral transmissions are: Mahamudra, Father Tantra, Mother Tantra, and Clear Light. Tilopa also had the transmission of Mahamudra directly from Buddha Vajradhara in a pure vision.

Tilopa's principle disciple was the Kashmiri master Naropa. Naropa studied Sutra and Tantra extensively at Nalanda University, but then left to seek out a realized master who could help him stabilize his mind. Having met Tilopa, Naropa underwent twelve years of intense hardships. Naropa received special Vajrayana pith instructions from Tilopa for attaining Buddhahood in one body and one lifetime. At the end, the supreme realization of Mahamudra dawned directly in Naropa's mind. These teachings form the foundation of the Drukpa Kagyu lineage.

The lineage passed from Naropa to the Tibetan translator Marpa, and then to Marpa's disciple, the renowned yogi Milarepa. From Milarepa, the lineage passed to his chief disciples, the yogi Rechungpa and Gampopa the monk. From Gampopa, it passed to Pagmo Drupa, who spread the teachings widely, and founded the eight subsidiary Kagyu schools. In the case of the Drukpa Kagyu, the lineage passed from Pagmo Drupa to Lingchen Repa. Lingchen Repa's chief disciple was Tsangpa Gyare, who founded the Drukpa

Kagyu lineage. Tsangpa Gyare had many disciples, and from him the three main lineages of Upper, Lower, and Middle Drukpa spread and flourished. There was a prophecy that the Drukpa teachings would spread as far as a vulture could fly in eighteen days, and indeed the Drukpa spread widely throughout Tibet and the Himalayan regions.

THE MAIN INSTRUCTIONS

The main instructions of the Drukpa lineage were compiled and arranged by Tsangpa Gyare, the founder of the lineage. Tsangpa Gyare said that in his lineage, the view comes from Gampopa's tradition, the pith instructions from Rechungpa, and the special teaching on interdependence (*tendrel*) from a pure vision he had in meditation. In general, the teachings are described in terms of two mutually supportive paths—the path of skillful means and the path of liberation. Being a direct and unelaborate approach, Mahamudra belongs to the path of liberation. The complete practice tradition that developed in the main monasteries of the Drukpa Kagyu is known as the "five special teachings of the Drukpa Kagyu."

1. The view is Mahamudra.
2. The meditation is the Six Practices of Naropa.
3. The conduct is the Six Cycles of Equal Taste.
4. The fruition is the Seven Supreme Interdependencies.
5. The most cherished of them all is the profound path of Guru Yoga.

1. The View Is Mahamudra

The view of Mahamudra refers to the direct realization of empty lucidity, the nature of mind. The term "view" here indicates this is the most crucial understanding, the essential realization of the nature of everything. Mahamudra also refers to the approach of realizing that natural state. The meaning of "mahamudra," or

chakgya chenpo in Tibetan, is expressed by this explanation in the
Vajra Verses of the Hearing Lineage:

> *Chak*—recognizing the essence of nondual timeless
>   awareness,
> *Gya*—the knots of samsara are freed,
> *Chenpo*—born only from the lamp of unity, it does not
>   come from anywhere else;
> It is the originally free dharmakaya.

In general, the view does not relate to the object that is perceived
but rather to the perceiving awareness. The view of Mahamudra is
to seal all phenomena of samsara and nirvana within the union of
bliss and emptiness, and practice in the sustained continuity of that
state. In the case of Mahamudra, the perceiver is self-knowing nondual awareness. During the practice of meditation, which at this
stage is deliberate, the practitioner begins with the experience of
an apparent mahamudra, not the mahamudra itself. By continuing
the practice, eventually the meditator comes to the realization of
actual mahamudra and can truly rest in uncontrived naturalness.

2. The Meditation Is the Six Practices of Naropa

The main meditation practices of the path of skillful means are
the six practices of Naropa, which organize the special teachings
Naropa received from Tilopa. These are: inner heat (*tummo*), illusory body, dream yoga, clear light, *bardo*, and transference (*powa*).
These profound and secret Vajrayana practices work with perception and the subtle energies of the body to transform the ordinary
body and ordinary perceptions into a wisdom body and pure
perception.

3. The Conduct is the Six Cycles of Equal Taste

The Six Cycles of Equal Taste is a special set of unique teachings of the Drukpa Kagyu. Equal taste refers to the subject, and means that the perceiver experiences everything as equal in "taste," meaning free of hope and fear and other mental constructs. Generally speaking, the practice of equal taste is called "reverse meditation," because instead of rejecting afflictions, conceptual thoughts, and so forth, in equal taste practice they are taken as the path. While meditation is the path, equal taste is the result. This approach is considered very effective but only suitable to be taught to mature practitioners. The six cycles of equal taste are:

- Thoughts
- Afflictive emotions
- Gods and demons
- Suffering
- Sickness
- Death

The story of the six cycles of equal taste begins with Dharma Dode, the son of Marpa, who passed away as a young man. He had already mastered the practice of transference and so while dying transferred his consciousness into a pigeon and flew to a charnel ground in India. He found the body of a young boy who had just passed away and transferred his consciousness into the boy's body. This boy became the mahasiddha Tipupa.

Milarepa's disciple Rechungpa went to India, studied with Tipupa, and received the teachings on the six cycles of equal taste. Tipupa told Rechungpa that the time was not right to spread these teachings, but rather that Rechungpa should conceal them and that three generations later a worthy disciple in the lineage would discover them. Tsangpa Gyare, founder of the Drukpa lineage, who lived three generations after Rechungpa, discovered these teachings in a rock in a border area between Tibet and Bhutan. Tsangpa Gyare practiced these teachings and transmitted them to his disciples and they became a special and integral part of the Drukpa tradition.

4. The Result Is the Seven Supreme Interdependencies

While meditating under a tree, Tsangpa Gyare had a vision of seven buddhas, and received the teaching known as the seven supreme interdependencies. The main meaning of these teachings is connected to the unity of emptiness and interdependence. This is the core teaching of all the Buddhist vehicles.

5. The Most Cherished of Them All Is Guru Yoga

Through practicing guru yoga well, and generating intense devotion to one's master and the lineage, powerful blessings are received. These blessings become an enhancement of all the other practices, including the view, meditation, conduct, and result. The guru yoga and blessings are considered the essential, indispensable aspects of all the other practices, and thus are said to be the most cherished of them all. In general, all lineages practice guru yoga and cherish the spiritual master, but the Drukpa Kagyu places an especially strong emphasis on these elements.

SPECIAL PITH INSTRUCTION: THE THREE FIERCE MANTRAS OF THE DRUKPA KAGYU

Tsangpa Gyare used three short phrases to train his mind to relate to all sorts of situations. The phrases became a beloved part of the Drukpa transmission and are known as the "Three Fierce Mantras" of the Drukpa Kagyu. They are profound points expressed in very ordinary language, meant to cut straight to the bone:

- Whatever happens, let it happen!
- However things go, let them go!
- There is no need of anything!

Conclusion

My teachers Khamtrul Rinpoche, Adeu Rinpoche, and the *togdens* (yogis) of Tashi Jong Monastery in India received Drukpa Mahamudra teachings and practiced them. I also received these instructions and have found them very rich and useful for my own practice. I encouraged Gerardo, Sean, and Adam to translate a selection of Mahamudra from the Drukpa lineage so more people could benefit from them. One great master of this tradition, Dorzong Rinpoche, recently passed away and remained for almost three weeks in *tukdam* (a continuous meditative state after passing away), displaying the power of having brought these practices to fruition. This is not just a tradition of the past. The yogic tradition in Tashi Jong is still alive and thriving. The yogis uphold and embody these teachings, so Drukpa Mahamudra is a living lineage of practice and realization.

Aspiration

I pray that these teachings inspire many beings to take up the profound practice of Mahamudra and realize the natural state of mind. May great compassion dawn and benefit countless beings who realize their nature as Mahamudra.

Tsoknyi Rinpoche
January 2017

The Supreme Siddhi
of Mahamudra

Tilopa (988–1069)

Born to a Brahmin family in Bengal, Tilopa became an ascetic at a young age. Later, while meditating in a tiny grass hut, he received transmission directly from the Dharmakaya Buddha Vajradhara. Tilopa also received tantric lineages from human masters, and became a mahasiddha and the main source of the Mahamudra and tantric teachings for the Kagyu lineage.

Ganges Mahamudra

Pith Instructions to Naropa

Tilopa

IN SANSKRIT: *Mahāmudropadeśa*
IN TIBETAN: *Phyag rgya chen po'i man ngag*

I bow down to the glorious innate wisdom!

Mahamudra cannot be taught.
Yet you, intelligent Naropa, have undergone hardships,
And through devotion to your guru have endured suffering,
Keep these words in your heart, O fortunate one!

Kye ho!
Look deeply at the things of the world;
Like a dream or an illusion, they cannot last.
Dreams and illusions have no basis in reality,
So muster weariness for them and give up worldly affairs.

Leave behind your entourage of close ones and servants—
All those objects of attachment and anger.
Meditate alone in solitary places—forest or mountain retreats.
Remain continuously in nonmeditation.
If nonattainment is attained, this is attaining mahamudra.

Samsaric things are meaningless, the cause of grief.
Constructed things have no essence, so look at the ultimate!

The intellect cannot see the meaning beyond concepts.
Deliberate activity cannot acquire the meaning of non-doing.
If you want to secure the meaning of non-doing beyond concepts,
Cut the root of mind and let awareness rest nakedly.

Clarify the murky water of thoughts.
Do not block or believe in appearances, just leave them be.
When there is no accepting or rejecting, mind is freed within
   mahamudra.

A flourishing tree is full of branches, leaves, and flowers,
But all its foliage shrivels once the root is cut.
Like how the darkness of one thousand eons
Is dispelled by a single torch,
A single moment of mind's luminosity
Completely clears an eon's worth of obscurations and misdeeds.

Those whose minds are less lucid,
Who cannot abide in the essential meaning,
Should grasp the vital points of the wind energies,
And let awareness be in its essence.
They should exert themselves with various gazes and
   concentration techniques
Until awareness remains in its natural state.

When examining the core of space,
All clinging to a center or edge will cease.
Likewise, when mind examines mind
The throngs of thoughts cease, and it becomes nonconceptual.
Then you will see the nature of unsurpassable awakening.

Vapors rise from the earth, form clouds, and then disperse in
   the sky.
They have not gone anywhere, nor do they remain anywhere.

Billowing thoughts that come from the mind are just the same:
Once seen as your very own mind, the waves of thoughts disperse.

Space is beyond having color or shape,
Untainted by black or white—unchanging.
Likewise, one's mind is beyond color and shape
And cannot be blemished by virtue and negativity.
The pure luminous essence of the sun
Cannot be obscured by the darkness of a thousand eons.
In the same way, eons of samsara cannot obscure
The luminous essence of mind.

Even if we designate space to be empty,
We still cannot express how space is.
Likewise, even though we say the mind is luminous,
That neither proves its existence nor its relation to anything else.

In space, does anything rely on anything?
Similarly, your mahamudra mind has no object of support.

Rest at ease in the uncontrived natural state!
If your bonds loosen,
There is no doubt you will be free.
The nature of mind is thus like space.
All phenomena without exception are included in that.

Drop all physical activity and rest in naturalness.
Let your speech be without much talking and chatting, it is all
    just echoes!
Do not direct the mind to ordinary thoughts,
Give attention to the Dharma of fulfillment.

Like a bamboo shaft, the body has no core.
The mind is like the center of space, beyond mental constructs.

In that state there is nothing to grasp or reject, so rest at ease.
The mind without reference point is mahamudra.
By habituating to that, unsurpassable awakening is attained.

Without an object to focus on, the nature of mind is lucid.
Having no path to traverse is entering the Buddha's path.
By habituating to nonmeditation,
Supreme enlightenment is achieved.

The king of views transcends all forms of grasper and grasped.
The king of meditation is nondistraction.
The king of conduct is effortlessness.
When there is no hope and fear, the fruition manifests.

The unborn all-ground is devoid of patterns and obscuring
     covers.
Do not distinguish between meditation and breaks,
Rest in the unborn essence!

All that appears is your own perception.
Conceptual phenomena are exhausted.
The supreme king of views is completely free of all extremes.
The supreme king of meditation is limitless, deep and open.
The supreme king of conduct is effortless, self-sustaining.
The supreme king of fruition is free of hope, naturally abiding.

The activity for a beginner is like a rushing canyon stream:
In the middle, it flows slowly like the Ganges River.
At the end, it is like a small river joining the sea,
The meeting of mother and child.

Having your own texts and philosophical positions,
Being able to speak of many Dharmas;
The tantras, paramitas, vinaya, and so forth,
Will not result in seeing the luminous mahamudra.

Do not engage the mind and you will be free of all your heart's
    desires,
Which are self-arising and self-subsiding, just like waves on water.
Through the arising of desire, luminosity is obscured and not seen.

The real meaning of precepts, vows, and *samayas*
Is violated by concepts.
If you do not settle, do not fixate, and do not stray from the
    profound meaning,
This is the practice of sublime beings, a lamp in the darkness.

If you are free of all wishes and desires
And do not abide in any extreme,
You will see all the Dharmas of the Three Baskets.

If you dedicate yourself to the meaning of this,
You will be free from the prison of samsara.
Stable meditation on this truth will burn up ignorance,
Misdeeds, and obscurations.
What I have explained is called
"The lamp of the teachings."

All those foolish beings uninterested in this truth
Will be exhausted, carried endlessly by the river of samsara.
The torments of the lower realms are unbearable, how sad!
Those who want to be free of sorrow should rely on a skillful
    master.
By receiving the blessings, their minds will be liberated.

If you rely on a *karmamudra*,
The wisdom of bliss and emptiness appears.
Through the blessed union of means and wisdom,
Let the drop descend slowly, hold it, then reverse and draw it up.

Guide it to the sacred centers and
Pervade it throughout the body.
If there is no attachment to this,
The empty bliss of wakefulness will dawn.

You will have a long life, free of gray hairs, and be lustrous like
    the moon.
You will have a clear and radiant complexion
And have the power of a lion.
Having quickly attained the common *siddhis*,
You will reach the supreme.

May this instruction on the key points of Mahamudra
Be kept in the hearts of fortunate beings!

This completes the instructions by the glorious Tilopa given to
Naropa on the bank of the Ganges River.

May it be virtuous![4]

Condensed Verses of Mahamudra

Naropa

IN SANSKRIT: *Mahāmudrāsaṃjñāsaṃhitā*
IN TIBETAN: *Phyag rgya chen po'i tshig bsdus pa*

I pay homage to the continuity of great bliss!

The Mahamudra view of appearances, awareness, and unity are taught:

1. The Meaning of the Mahamudra of Appearances

As for the expression of mahamudra,
All phenomena are your own mind.
Seeing outer things as real is confusion;
Like a dream, they are empty of essence.

2. The Mahamudra of Awareness

The mind, moreover, is merely the movement of thoughts and
  memories;
It has no nature; it is the dynamism of wind energy.
Empty of essence, it is like space;
All phenomena are like space, abiding as great equality.

Naropa (1016–1100)

The mahapandita Naropa was a great scholar from Kashmir. He
mastered Buddhist studies at Nalanda University, but then left to
seek a master who could teach him how to tame his mind. Naropa
underwent twelve years of intense hardships under Tilopa's guidance,
and finally attained complete mahamudra realization.

3. The Mahamudra of Unity

As for expressing mahamudra,
Its essence cannot be taught.
Therefore, the suchness of mind
Is the very continuity of mahamudra.

There are also three types of Mahamudra meditation:

1. Mahamudra's Natural Way of Abiding

The nature of mahamudra is uncontrived and unchanging.
Whoever sees and realizes this
Experiences all that appears as mahamudra,
For the great dharmakaya is all-pervasive.

2. The Way of Realizing Mahamudra

Rest loosely in the uncontrived nature;
The dharmakaya cannot be fathomed.
When you rest without searching, this is meditation;
To search while meditating is confusion.

3. The Mahamudra of Indivisibility

Because it is free of meditating and not meditating,
How could there be separation or non-separation from that state?
A yogi realizes everything to be like space and magical displays.

The conduct of Mahamudra again has three aspects:

1. The Mahamudra of Self-Liberation

All virtuous and negative karma will be liberated
By knowing their suchness.

Afflictions are great wisdom
And, like a fire that benefits a forest,
Are a yogi's boon.

2. The Mahamudra of One Taste

How could there truly be going or remaining?
What kind of meditation
Results from traveling to solitary places?
Whoever does not realize suchness,
Aside from having temporary experiences, will not be liberated.

3. The Mahamudra of Inseparability

If you realize suchness, what can bind you?
Except for remaining undistracted in that state,
There is nothing to meditate on:
There is neither a resting nor a nonresting in equipoise.
This practice cannot be created or improved by an antidote.

Once again, the fruition of Mahamudra has three sections:

1. The Mahamudra of All That Appears and Exists

In this, nothing whatsoever is accomplished—
Appearances self-liberated are the basic space of phenomena.
Thoughts self-liberated are great wisdom,
The nondual equality of dharmakaya.

2. The Mahamudra beyond Samsara

Like the continuous flow of a mighty river,
Whatever you do is meaningful.
This is the great bliss of Buddhahood,
Where samsara has no place.

3. The Ultimate Mahamudra

All phenomena are empty of their own essence.
The mind that grasps the notion of "empty"
Is self-purified.
Free from concepts, without mental fabrication—
This is the path of all the buddhas.

Final Advice and Dedication

For those most fortunate beings,
My heart advice is here collected into words.
Through this, may all beings without exception
Reside in mahamudra!

This instruction was given orally from the great master Naropa to Marpa Chökyi Lodro at Pushpahari.

Śubham astu sarvajagatām!

These thirteen verses summarize all aspects of Mahamudra without exception. The purpose and divisions of this teaching should be understood from a detailed oral explanation, in accordance with its essential meaning.

Do not put your confidence in mixed-up versions. This was written according to the authentic ancient manuscripts, so do not think it has been distorted.

Marpa Chökyi Lodro (1012–1096)

The first Tibetan in this lineage, Marpa was a great translator who traveled to India and Nepal several times to receive teachings and transmissions, mainly from Naropa and Maitripa. He was a married householder yogi and brought many transmissions to Tibet.

A Vision of Saraha

*The Essential Importance of the Uncreated
Meaning of the Four Syllables of Mahamudra:
A Pith Instruction Expressed in a Vajra Song*

Marpa

*The pith instruction, the essence of the uncreated found in the mean-
ing of the four syllables of Mahamudra, was revealed to Lord Marpa
by the song of Saraha.*

At this auspicious and glorious time of the waxing moon of the
tenth day, during a *ganachakra* feast of the *dakas*, you, prince of
Lokya, with unwavering samaya, have asked me to sing a song never
heard before.

I have traveled on a long road and I am exhausted, so this song
will not be much. I am also unskilled in the art of composition.
Nevertheless, because no one is more important than you, my
friend, and since I cannot turn down the request of an important
man, I will sing a wondrous song, something never heard before, a
song of Lord Brahmin. All of you practitioners of Sutra and Mantra gathered here listen well and keep it in your hearts.

Last spring during the third month of the lunar calendar, I traveled up from central Nepal. After having been on the road for the
length of a having a meal, I arrived at the tax station in a town of
low-caste people. The tax collectors exploit all who they meet and
detain defenseless Tibetan travelers, and they held me against my
will for several days.

One night in a light sleep I dreamt that two actual Brahmin

girls, wearing the Brahmin thread, appeared before me. They smiled coyly with sidelong glances and said, "You must go to Shri Parvata in the south."

I replied, "I have not been there before and do not know the way."

"Brother, you need not do anything difficult. We shall carry you there on our shoulders."

They seated me upon a cloth palanquin, which they raised into the sky like a parasol. In a flash, I arrived at Shri Parvata in the south. There, in the cool shade of a grove of fig trees, on a *tira* corpse seat flanked by two queens, sat the Great Brahmin, Saraha.

Never before had I seen such majestic brilliance. He was adorned with charnel ground attire and beamed with delight.

"Welcome, son," he said.

Seeing the lord, I was overcome with joy. The hairs on my body stood on end and I was moved to tears. I circumambulated him seven times and offered full prostrations. I placed the soles of his feet upon my crown and supplicated him, "Father, hold me in your compassion!"

He blessed my body with his. The moment he placed his hand upon my head, my body, like that of a drunken elephant, was intoxicated with uncontaminated bliss and an experience of immutability dawned within me.

He blessed my speech with his. He unveiled the meaning of the four syllables, the lion's roar of emptiness, and, like the dream of a mute, an experience beyond words dawned within me.

He blessed my mind with his and I realized the dharmakaya, that which neither comes nor goes, and within me dawned the experience of having no thoughts, like that of a corpse in a charnel ground.

The pure speech of great bliss arose from the vase of his precious throat as he sang with a Brahmin's melody this vajra song, pointing out things as they are—essentially an empty sky free of clouds. Thus, I heard the unborn self-utterance:

"*Namo!* Compassion and emptiness are inseparable.
The uninterrupted flow of the innate mind
Is suchness, primordially pure.
Space is seen in union with space
Because the root resides at home;
Mental consciousness is imprisoned.

"Meditating upon this, subsequent thoughts
Are not patched together in the mind.
Knowing that everything is of the nature of mind,
Meditation requires no additional remedy.
The nature of mind cannot be thought of,
So rest in the natural state.

"When you see this, you will be liberated.
Just as a child would follow the behavior of savages,
Be carefree, eat flesh, be a madman.
Be like a fearless lion,
Let your elephant mind wander free.

"As the bee hovers over flowers,
Do not view samsara as defiled;
There is no nirvana to attain.
This is the way of the natural state:
Rest in uncontrived freshness.
Do not think of activities and do not be partial,
Look toward the center of the sky—utter simplicity.

"To go beyond the exhaustion of phenomena
Is essential;
This is the summit of views, mahamudra."

This meaning of symbols, which pierces the heart, I heard from the
mouth of the Great Brahmin.

At that very moment I awoke and with the iron hook of recollection I snared the song's essence, never to forget. Within the darkness of bewildered sleep the vision of insight had opened and, like the sun rising, cleared away the darkness of confusion. I thought that even if I were to meet with the buddhas of the three times, I would have nothing to ask them. This was the decisive experience of mind itself, the experience that banishes all discursive thought. Amazing!

Eh ma! Although I have been told not to speak about the prophecies of the *yidams* and *dakinis*, as well as the profound truth spoken by the guru, tonight I cannot help myself. Except for this evening, I have never before spoken of these things. I have now revealed them as you have heard.

I am a man who has traveled a long way without friends or relatives. Now, when I am fatigued, my son, what you have done for me I will not forget—it is etched into my mind. Heart friend, your kindness is repaid.

Gurus who are the lords who dwell above, yidams who bestow accomplishments, and *dharmapalas* who clear obstacles, please refrain from scolding me and forgive me if I have made any mistakes.

The meaning here is as follows: The first syllable represents the dharmakaya, the second is the complete and perfect *sambhogakaya*, the third is the *nirmanakaya*, and the last syllable, the fourth, is the *svabhavikakaya*.

Mahamudra, the great seal, refers to the four Dharmas of the ground, path, and fruition. They are explained at the time of the path as: (1) cutting the root of mind, (2) explaining the methods for the mind's resting, (3) abandoning the mind's hidden flaws, and (4) proceeding along the path.

This is the heart practice of Marpa, the renowned four syllables of Mahamudra.

The Illuminating Wisdom

Milarepa

Homage to the accomplished masters!

These instructions are said to have originated from the master Tilopa. They passed through the learned Naropa to Marpa of Lodrak. I, the yogi of Gungthang, served this master with faith and devotion for a long time and he in his great compassion passed these teachings on to me. I meditated on them and earnestly applied myself to their practice with great diligence. I received their blessings and the physical inner heat blazed so strong that I did not have much need for clothes.

Once during a practice session, the mind's natural luminosity arose within me. I then grasped all the unique and quite extraordinary features of the numerous, unpolluted tantras together with their pith instructions sequentially through the natural state of things, the path to its realization, and the result. The natural state of things is mahamudra, which can be more extensively described in terms of the ground of mahamudra, path of mahamudra, and fruition of mahamudra.

Firstly, the natural state, the mind of the Buddha, is the nature of being sentient. It is not established as having any color or shape, or having a center or boundary. It is beyond fragmentation and preference and is neither experienced as existent nor nonexistent; it is neither confused nor liberated; it did not arise from a cause nor is it changed by conditions; the Buddha's teaching does not change it, nor does the confusion of beings alter it; it is neither improved by realization nor impaired by bewilderment.

The path of mahamudra is the practice that enables the

Milarepa (1040–1123)

The great yogi Jetsun Milarepa endured severe ordeals while training under Marpa to purify his karma. Milarepa is renowned for his total renunciation and for attaining full enlightenment in one lifetime. His remarkable life story and his thousands of spiritual songs are among the most beloved in Tibetan Buddhist literature.

realization of the ground. As such, one should apply the following: when placing the mind, place it without a reference point; when settling the mind, settle it without distraction; when thinking, think without fixation; when a thought arises, allow it to arise as suchness; and allow liberation to occur naturally.

The fruition of mahamudra is free from "something that liberates" and "something which is liberated"; it is beyond hope and fear; it is said to be the exhaustion of mental states and phenomena; it is ungraspable, beyond the mind, and indescribable.

The three—ground, path, and fruition—are to be practiced together.

Gampopa (1079–1153)

Initially a talented physician, Gampopa became a monk and then one of the two chief disciples of Milarepa. He synthesized the Kadam Mahayana teachings of Atisha with the oral instructions on yogic practice and Mahamudra from Milarepa to form the Kagyu lineage. Gampopa had many great disciples including the first Karmapa and Pagmo Drupa.

The Single Sufficient Path of Mahamudra

Gampopa

Homage to the sublime gurus!

This work includes three sections: (1) resolving the natural state, (2) pointing out the nature of things, and (3) training in suchness as the path.

1. Resolving the Natural State

Mahamudra has no cause.
Mahamudra has no condition.
Mahamudra has no method.
Mahamudra has no path.
Mahamudra has no result.

2. Pointing Out the Nature of Things

Mahamudra has no cause, yet faith and devotion are its cause.
Mahamudra has no condition, yet a sublime guru is its condition.
Mahamudra has no method, yet not fabricating is its method.
Mahamudra has no path, yet remaining undistracted is its path.
Mahamudra has no result, yet the mind liberated within the
    dharmata is its fruition.

3. Training in Suchness as the Path

As a preliminary, practice guru yoga with faith, devotion, and respect three times during the day and three times during the night. For the main practice, remain undistracted within the state of an uncontrived mind. As the conclusion, recognize that whatever appears is none other than your mind, and train your awareness accordingly.

Relying upon the sequential arising of experiences, exert yourself in meditation until mind is exhausted. Experiences can arise as either unfavorable or favorable. Unfavorable experiences arising from meditation include dullness, excitement, illness, fear, fright, doubt, and so forth. Recognize them to be fleeting experiences and, without seeking to abandon them, continue to meditate. Taking these very experiences as the objects of your practice will lead you to favorable experiences. Favorable experiences include an initial state of mental stillness. This will lead to an experience of the mind's empty nature, which will bring about realization and the turning away from attachment.

Based upon the sequential arising of experiences, exert yourself in meditation and do not be complacent: It is not enough for your mind to be still; you must meditate to see its essence. Mere recognition of the essence is not sufficient; you must continue meditating to realize it. Realization alone will not suffice; you must meditate further to reverse attachment. Simply reversing attachment is not enough; you must meditate until, liberating your mind within the dharmata, both mental states and phenomena are exhausted and you awaken to Buddhahood.

OFFERING REALIZATION

In the Presence of Pagmo Drupa

LINGCHEN REPA

Homage to the precious guru!

Lord, you told me to meditate on the innate essence,
And meditate is what I did;
It so happened that meditation and meditator simply vanished,
And there was no post-meditation to uphold.

Through the experience of the torch of *samadhi*,
I realized the mind as the dharmakaya, free of elaborations.
Thus, clinging to experiences simply vanished,
And there was no straying to eliminate.

Through none other than the mind resting as it is—
Without altering with remedies—
Doubts about "is it" or "is it not" simply vanished,
And there was no sense of discomfort left.

Like meeting a person known from before,
By recognizing thoughts as the dharmakaya,
Grasping to them as faults or qualities simply vanished,
And there was nothing to reject or accept.

Like the sun dawning upon darkness,
Realization arose from within.

Lingchen Repa Pema Dorje (1128–1188)

Also known as Druptob Napupa, Lingchen Repa studied medicine in his early years and also became skilled in black magic. He then studied Dharma with Lama Shang, Ra Lotsawa, and Lama Khyung Tsangpa. He later met Pagmo Drupa, disciple of Gampopa, and became a mahasiddha renowned for his renunciation and high realization.

Thus, philosophical assertions simply vanished,
And there were no words to speak.

By realizing that the guru and the buddhas of the three times
Are not different from my own mind,
Ordinary perception simply vanished,
And there was nothing to long for.

The bubble of illusory body is always destroyed.
As I realized that the mind is unborn and immortal,
The fear of death simply vanished,
And there was nothing to grieve about.

If we meet, I am in the presence of the lord.
If we do not, I wander aimlessly through mountain hermitages.
If hungry, I go for alms without attachment.
If cold, I warm myself with the heat of tummo.

If sad, I sing a song of spiritual experience.
If sick, I balance the elements.
I slash experiences of happiness or sorrow on the spot,
And go about my everyday life as I please.

Tsangpa Gyare (1161–1211)

The foremost disciple of Lingchen Repa, Tsangpa Gyare, was the founder of the Drukpa lineage. He discovered instructions hidden by Rechungpa, disciple of Milarepa, and also received special teachings in a vision of seven buddhas. From his chief disciples the Upper, Lower, and Middle Drukpa lineages spread. His activity to benefit beings was immense.

The Song of Confidence

Tsangpa Gyare

Homage to the precious one!

As I realize the emptiness of the mind,
Samsara and nirvana merge into the same essence,
And I do not even see anything to be accepted or rejected.
This is my confidence in the view.

When the mind rests unmodified it is the dharmakaya,
Fleeting thoughts are naturally liberated,
And the essential meaning is experienced without thinking.
This is my confidence in the meditation.

Perceptions of the six sense objects,
When not grasped, become self-liberated,
And I do not see dwelling on reference points.
This is my confidence in the conduct.

Mind essence, as pure as space,
Is not defiled by faults or ethical downfalls.
I do not see dwelling on observing moral boundaries.
This is my confidence in the samaya.

When this ordinary thought, as it is,
Is timelessly perceived as the dharmakaya,
The three kayas of the Buddha are spontaneously present.
This is my confidence in the fruition.

Realizing the primordially existing truth,
When the bubble of the illusory body bursts,
The mind turns into vivid, continuous dharmakaya.
This is my confidence in dying joyfully.

The lord guru, so kind!
A son born to the mother, so meaningful!
Possessing a human body, so excellent!
Fortunate ones, my mind is at ease!

The Song of Being Unbiased

The Second Drukchen Kunga Paljor

Invited from Echab Dzi to Tarkha hermitage, he said:
"Homage to mahamudra!"

Since I am not biased toward the view,
Primordial purity and spontaneous presence merge into one.
Fixation on eternalism or nihilism is naturally liberated.
What is the use of a biased view?

Since I am not biased toward the meditation,
Phenomena and emptiness merge into one.
Fixation on them as separate is naturally liberated.
What is the use of a biased meditation?

Since I am not biased toward the conduct,
Forbidden and permitted behaviors merge into one.
Grasping at the notions of undesirable and antidote is naturally
   liberated.
What is the use of a biased conduct?

Since I am not biased toward the fruition,
The immediate and ultimate merge into one.
Accomplisher and accomplished are naturally liberated.
What is the use of a biased fruition?

Since I am not biased toward philosophical tenets,
Self-emptiness and other-emptiness merge into one.

THE SONG OF BEING UNBIASED

THE SECOND DRUKCHEN KUNGA PALJOR

Invited from Echab Dzi to Tarkha hermitage, he said:
"Homage to mahamudra!"

Since I am not biased toward the view,
Primordial purity and spontaneous presence merge into one.
Fixation on eternalism or nihilism is naturally liberated.
What is the use of a biased view?

Since I am not biased toward the meditation,
Phenomena and emptiness merge into one.
Fixation on them as separate is naturally liberated.
What is the use of a biased meditation?

Since I am not biased toward the conduct,
Forbidden and permitted behaviors merge into one.
Grasping at the notions of undesirable and antidote is naturally
    liberated.
What is the use of a biased conduct?

Since I am not biased toward the fruition,
The immediate and ultimate merge into one.
Accomplisher and accomplished are naturally liberated.
What is the use of a biased fruition?

Since I am not biased toward philosophical tenets,
Self-emptiness and other-emptiness merge into one.

The Second Drukchen Kunga Paljor (1428–1476)

Recognized as the incarnation of Tsangpa Gyare, Kunga Paljor was known for his knowledge of philosophy and Sanskrit. He was also renowned for his direct teachings revealing the nature of mind. His three most outstanding disciples were known as the "three divine madmen," including Tsang Nyon Heruka, Unyon, and Drukpa Kunley.

The bondage of dualistic fixation is naturally liberated.
What is the use of biased tenets?

The unerring intent of the Victorious One
Can only be maintained unbiasedly.
I have no care for that which is biased.
Have this understanding, fortunate ones!

Bardo Supplication

The Second Drukchen Kunga Paljor

Namo mahāmudrāyā!

Comprehending all phenomena as illusory,
Free from impure illusion, you discovered the pure kayas.
Leader who guides illusory beings,
To your illusory form I go for refuge.

Lord who has an illusory body,
Bless me and all beings tricked by illusion,
So that, undeceived by illusory phenomena,
We recognize the nature of illusion.

At the time of discarding this transient illusory body,
Bless us so that by cutting all the ties of attachment, aversion, and
    grasping,
And resting naturally in the unfabricated essence of mind,
We may take death as the path.

At death, outer phenomena cease:
Sight and the rest of the five senses gradually stop,
And forms and the rest of the five objects dissolve one by one.
When this happens, bless us so that we recognize the stages of
    dissolution.

As earth, water, fire, and air dissolve into consciousness,
Vitality wanes, one is thirsty and the mouth and nose dry up.

Warmth fades, and one's breathing is short and rattling.
At that time, bless us so that we take the pain of dying as
    the path.

Consciousness dissolves into luminosity and the outer breath
    stops,
While the inner breath continues during the four instants:
Appearance, increase, attainment, and great luminosity.
Bless us so that we may recognize them, one by one.

The inner sign of appearance is like smoke, the outer sign
    resembles a rising moon,
And the thirty-three concepts deriving from aggression subside.
Bless us so that, at this time,
We remain clear, alert, and determined.

The inner sign of increase is like fireflies, the outer sign like the
    rising sun,
And the forty concepts deriving from passion subside.
Bless us so that, at this time,
Aware and mindful, we recognize them.

The inner sign of attainment is like a burning lamp,
The outer sign is blackness, like an eclipse,
And the seven concepts deriving from ignorance subside.
Bless us so that, at this time, we recognize all with perfect
    attention.

When the fourth instant, the great luminosity, dawns,
The inner sign is like a cloudless sky,
The outer sign is like the break of day.
Bless us so that, at this time, mother and child luminosity merge.

If consciousness does not rest there but instead shifts
To the navel, in between eyebrows, cranium, nose, ears,

Eyes, urinary tract, anus, or mouth,
Bless us so as to block these nine and open the one exit.

Gods of the desire, form, and formless realms, *yakshas, kinnaras,*
Humans, animals, hell beings, or ghosts,
Bless us so that we close the doors to rebirth as these,
And dakas and dakinis welcome us into the celestial realm.

If consciousness were to wander in the bardo,
Then, not knowing we are dead, we will despair of relatives
    and friends
Who do not respond even though we want to relate to them,
Bless us so that, at that time, the ties of attachment and aversion
    are severed.

When, endowed with full sense faculties and miraculous karmic
    power,
We may go anywhere unimpeded,
Except to Mount Meru, Vajrasana, and one's mother's womb.
Bless us so that we may know it all to be an illusion.

The sun and moon are invisible and the body casts no shadow.
Just by thinking, one can go around the billion solar systems,
Helpless, like a feather blown about by the wind.
When this happens, bless us in order to master our own minds.

One feeds on smells, and the mind rapidly flickers.
When myriad deluded experiences occur,
And afraid and sad, we become depressed;
Bless us so that we recognize these to be delusions.

At times, one's memory is extremely clear,
But immediately one forgets
And doubts whether one is dead or alive.
When this happens, bless us so that we know we are
    unequivocally dead.

Three and a half days after death,
One realizes one is dead,
And, depressed and disheartened, seeks a refuge.
Bless us in order to know, at that time, our own awareness will be
    the refuge.

When we realize that state is the bardo,
Visualizing our body as the deity, then meditating on luminosity,
And further meditating on their indivisibility,
Bless us so that, by this, the pure illusory form arises.

When terrified by collapsing mountains, raging oceans, blazing
    forests,
And the sound resembling the howling gale at the end of times,
Roaring together with a thousand thunders,
Bless us so that we may perceive these as the natural sounds of
    reality.

When the five colored light rays mix and shine,
And from what seems like spheres of light of all sizes
Appear terrifying wrathful forms roaring orders to strike
    and kill,
Bless us so that we perceive these, our own projections, as the
    deity.

When, terrified, we feel we are plummeting,
Into the abyss of the whiteness, redness, and blackness,
Arising from passion, aggression, and ignorance,
Bless us so that we perceive this, our own projections, as pure.

When the body of our next birth takes form,
And the white, red, yellow, blue, and black lights
Of gods, humans, animals, pretas, and hell beings appear,
Bless us so that we know these five pathways one by one.

When we sees gods enjoying pleasures in celestial palaces,
Lakes adorned with swans, royal bulls and horses,
And in a mansion our parents in union,
Bless us so that attraction, aversion, and jealousy are purified.

When, driven by gale, rain, clouds, heat, and cold,
We approach a cave, a ravine, a wooden log, and so forth,
And feel like entering them to find refuge,
Bless us so that we know these to be bad places for rebirth.

Seeing houses of slaughter, fire or iron,
Attracted to them, we feel like entering,
Bless us so that we recognize our own nature and be fearless,
And so turn away from these bad places for rebirth.

When we have envy and jealousy in the case of birth through a
    womb or egg,
Attraction to smell and taste in the case of birth by warmth and
    moisture,
Or attachment to the places of miraculous birth,
Bless us so that we have no desire, aversion, or craving.

When seeing one's parents, or the other modes of birth,
Bless us so that, free of attraction or aversion, knowing it to be
    illusory,
And remembering the recognition of the natural state,
Without clinging, we close the door to the womb.

If, unsuccessful, we are to take birth.
Bless us so that, upon remembering,
We are born in Sukhavati, Tushita, or Abhirati,
Or as a *chakravartin* or in the Brahmin caste.

As soon as we are born, may we remember our previous life,
And have the fortune of practicing the Mahayana Dharma.

Through love, may we generate the purely altruistic attitude,
And, persevering, quickly attain enlightenment.

By the blessing power of the buddhas and bodhisattvas,
The pure nature of absolute reality,
And also our pure wishes,
May we achieve these aspirations as expressed.[5]

The Song of Not All

Drukpa Kunleg

I bow joyously!

Not all those who have memorized texts are called scholars;
A scholar is someone who knows the figurative and true meaning
   of the Dharma.
Not all those who know about all kinds of magic are called
   siddhas;
A siddha is someone who has realized the genuine natural state.
Not all those with squinting warm-looking eyes are called
   bodhisattvas;
A bodhisattva is someone who totally turns away from
   selfishness.
Not all those who sport a goatee are called *tantrikas*;
A tantrika is someone who has realized the phenomenal world as
   the deity.
Not all those who stay on a mountaintop strolling around are
   called full-time meditators;
If one's environment has become the clear light, one is a full-time
   meditator.
Not all those who behave ostensibly carefree are called realized
   yogis;
When one can stay in the natural state without interruption, one
   is a realized yogi.
To have a one-sided grasp of emptiness is not what is called the
   view;
Being without limitations or falling into extremes, that is the view.

Drukpa Kunleg (1455–1529)

The most renowned of the "enlightened madmen," Drukpa Kunleg
wandered through Tibet and Bhutan, scolding insincere monks,
teasing people, performing miracles, helping beings, and generally
behaving in outrageous ways. The stories of his hilarious and
amazing exploits are greatly loved in the Tibetan world.

To hold a "good" reference point as paramount is not what is
called meditation;
When there is no reference point and attributes are dropped, that
is meditation.
To pretend to be disciplined and have a double life is not what is
called conduct;
Conduct is to completely purify transgressions.
To build a nice place of practice is not what is called the fruition;
If one realizes the primordial spontaneous perfection, that is the
fruition.
To be satisfied with only conventional designations is not what is
called a geshe;
A geshe is someone who knows the inner meaning of words.
To only wear saffron robes is not what is called monk;
Monk means to be disciplined in body, speech, and mind.
Someone who irritates spirits is not what is called a practitioner
of *chöd*;
The practitioner of chöd is someone who cuts off deluded
perceptions.
To give food that was obtained sinfully does not make one a
sponsor;
When one applies the three doors to virtue, one is a sponsor.
To reveal the mandala for the sake of profit is not what is called
empowerment;
Empowerment is to establish worthy disciples in maturation and
liberation.
To collect desirable food and drink is not what is called the
sacred feast of ganachakra;
Ganachakra means to make the symbolic offerings of the
warriors.
To spout hundreds of words is not what is meant by explanation;
If one knows the six extremes and the four styles, that is
explanation.
To translate colloquial language into Tibetan is not what is called
a translation;

If one captures the wisdom mind of the victorious ones, one is a
translator.
To put bits of butter on the beer jar is not what is meant by
auspicious coincidence;
If all phenomena are known to be interdependent, that is
auspicious coincidence.
To say "may it be" or "may it happen," is not what is called
aspiration;
When the three spheres are not conceptualized, that is aspiration.

Notes on Mahamudra

Pema Karpo

I prostrate to the precious Kagyu!

This is an explanation of the instructions on the means for realizing the co-emergent mahamudra, which reveals the stream of the ordinary mind as perfect wisdom. It is divided into (1) the introduction, (2) the main practice, and (3) the conclusion.

INTRODUCTION

The introduction consists of the (1) ordinary preliminary practices and (2) extraordinary preliminary practices.

I. Ordinary Preliminary Practices

These have been explained elsewhere.

II. Extraordinary Preliminary Practices

Carry out the special preliminaries, from taking refuge and developing bodhichitta through to practicing guru yoga. Then, as it is said in the *Enlightenment of Vairochana Tantra* (*Vairochana Abhisambodhi Tantra*):

Straighten the body and adopt the vajra posture.
Rest the mind one-pointedly in mahamudra.[6]

Pema Karpo (1527–1592)

One of the greatest scholars of the Drukpa lineage, Pema Karpo was the fourth Drukchen Rinpoche. His writings fill dozens of volumes on history, philosophy, ritual, and Mahamudra. He is renowned in Tibet for his unbiased scholarship, sophistication, and profound commentaries on Sutra, Tantra, and Mahamudra.

Cross the legs in the vajra posture; place the hands below the navel in the gesture of evenness; straighten the spine; open the shoulders; bend the throat like a hook with a slight pressure on the adam's apple; direct the tongue to the upper palate. In general, attention is dominated by the senses and particularly by the eyes. Therefore, without closing or moving them, look straight ahead at a distance of about a yoke's length. These are what is known as the seven factors of Vairochana.

In terms of their function, these constitute the five factors of meditative concentration, by means of which the five wind-energies (*prana*) enter the central channel (*nadi*). Thus, the "clearing downward" energy enters the central channel by crossing the legs in the vajra posture; the same happens with the "accompanying fire" energy through the gesture of evenness, the "pervasive" energy through the open shoulders and erect spine, the "moving upwards" energy through the throat bent forwards, and the "life-holding" energy through the gaze and the tongue touching the upper palate. Once these five energies have entered the central channel, the different karmic energies (*karma prana*) follow, after which thought-free wisdom arises. This is called the isolated body, immobile body, and the body resting naturally. As for speech, expel the stale breath and remain silent. This is called the isolated speech, immobile speech, and the speech resting naturally.

Do not recall the past, do not imagine the future, and do not deliberately make up your meditation with concepts. Also, do not consider emptiness as nothingness. In the present moment, do not study what is perceived by the five senses by thinking, "it is this," or "it is not this." Turn the mind inward and, remaining as carefree as an infant, rest the mind in its natural flow, without even an instant of distraction.

> If you abandon all thoughts and thinking completely,
> Remain carefree like an infant,

And reverently keep your guru's instructions and exert
  yourself,
There is no doubt that the co-emergence will dawn.

Tilopa said:

Do not recall, do not imagine, do not examine,
Do not meditate, do not think;
Rest in the natural flow.

And the King of Dharma Youthful Moonlight (Gampopa) said:

Nondistraction is the path of all buddhas.

This is what is known as the isolated mind, unwavering mind, and
the mind resting naturally. Nagarjuna said:

Lord, it has been taught exhaustively that focusing
  mindfulness on the body
Is the single path traversed by the sugatas.
Adhere to this and guard it.
When mindfulness degenerates, the entire Dharma will be
  destroyed.[7]

What is described in these verses is the mindfulness of "not wandering." As said in the *Abhidharma*:

Mindfulness is not to forget something with which one is
  acquainted.[8]

MAIN PRACTICE

The main practice is divided into (1) ordinary practice and (2) special practice.

I. Ordinary Practice

This includes (1) looking for the experience of shamatha, the root of meditation, and meditating on the yoga of one-pointedness, and (2) examining the root of stillness and movement, recognizing vipashyana, and meditating within the yoga of simplicity.

A. Looking for the Experience of Shamatha and the Yoga of One-Pointedness
1. Meditation with Support
a. Support Other Than the Breath

Impure support: adopting a pebble or small piece of wood as a support

Place a small pebble in front of you as a support for your focus. Look only at the pebble. Your mind should neither be scattered outside nor concentrated within. Visualize your guru on the crown of your head. Regarding him as the Buddha in person, supplicate with the four-line prayer called *manamkhama.*[9] Ask him for siddhis by saying, "May I attain the supreme siddhi of Mahamudra." Then dissolve him into yourself. Feel that his mind has merged with yours, and rest in that state for as long as you can. Practice in this way, consulting your guru about what occurs in your mind.

If you feel dull, raise your gaze and meditate in a place with a vast, open view. Apply the same to drowsiness, and tighten up with mindfulness. If agitated, sit in an isolated place with subdued light, lower the gaze, and emphasize relaxation.

Pure support: adopting the body, speech, and mind of the Tathagata as supports to meditation

Body: A representation of the form of the Buddha is taken as a support. Place before yourself a statue or a painting of the Buddha and steadfastly focus on it. Otherwise, visualize him in front of you. His body is yellow, like refined gold, and is adorned with the major and minor marks of excellence. It radiates light and is dressed in the three Dharma robes. Always keep this image present in your mind.

Speech: A letter is taken as a support. Visualize the letter HŪṂ in front of you. It is as if written with a single hair, and stands on a moon disc about the size of a thumbnail.

Mind: A *bindu* is taken as a support. Fixate your mind, as before, on a visualized egg-shaped sphere about the size of a pea that has the unique characteristic of radiating light.

b. The Breath as a Support

Vajra recitation as a support

Naturally rest the body and mind. Focus on the inhalations and exhalations of your breath and do not involve yourself with any other activity. Count the breaths—one, two . . . up to 21,600. Thus, one comes to know how many times the breath moves in and out.[10]

Next, while the breath is going in and out, follow it. Investigate whether it moves through the entire body or only one part of it. Through this, one comes to know the characteristics of the breath.[11]

Then, merge your awareness with the breath. The breath goes down from the tip of the nose to the navel, stays there, and comes back to the nose. Observe the nature of each of these states. Through this, one comes to see the color and length of each of the energies as they are.[12]

Next, examine each of the five major elements individually, whereby one comes to know the increase and decrease of the in and out movements of the breath.[13]

Then, turn the breath into a white OṂ while exhaling, a blue HŪṂ while inhaling, and a red ĀḤ while it stays. Through this, one actualizes the cessation of the in and out movements of the breath.[14]

The vase as a support

Expel the stale breath three times. Then, breathe in the upper air gently from the nostrils, draw up the lower air, and try to hold the breath for as long as you can.

The mind described as very difficult to tame does not exist apart from the wind-energy. Hence, as the shifting of the breath ceases, the thoughts that wander toward objects also come to an end.

2. Meditation Without Support

This includes (1) abruptly slashing sudden thoughts, (2) letting whatever arises be, and (3) highlighting the key points of the method of resting.

a. Abruptly Slashing Sudden Thoughts

Practicing as explained before, when the mind follows an object and a thought arises, tighten up through mindfulness and decide, "I will not indulge in the proliferation of thoughts and I must not allow even one thought to arise." Meditate in this way, swiftly and abruptly slashing the proliferation of sudden thoughts.

Practice, extending the periods of meditation, until thoughts become more and more numerous and finally arise one after the other in a seemingly uninterrupted stream. Known as identifying thoughts like recognizing the enemy, this is the first stillness, called "like a waterfall."

In other words, since the mind stays still an instant at a time, the arising and cessation of a thought is noticed. Because of this, it only seems that thoughts have increased in number. In fact, thoughts arise in a continuous stream; they neither increase nor decrease because it is the nature of thoughts to arise in one instant and cease in the following one.

b. Letting Whatever Arises Be

Let thoughts do what they will. Do not be carried away by them, do not stop them. Stabilize your mind like a vigilant observer. Practicing in this way, thoughts will have no way of proliferating, and your mind will remain one-pointedly still in shamatha meditation.

It will happen that thoughts of all kinds will again arise. If you continue to meditate as before, the stream of stillness will become longer and longer. This is the intermediate stillness, known as "like a river flowing gently."

Through this key point of loose resting, the impurities of the mind become separated from its pure aspect. As the Lord of Dharma (Tsangpa Gyare) said:

> When the mind is not altered, it is at ease.
> When water is not disturbed, it becomes limpid.

And the great Lord of Yogins (Lingchen Repa) stated:

> If you rest in natural freshness without modifying,
>   realization will dawn;
> Maintaining it like the flow of a river, it reaches completion.
> Totally abandon reference points and signs of one's own
>   being,
> And always rest in that state, yogin.

Also, Saraha declared, referring to these two types of meditation:

> When bound up, the mind starts to go in the ten directions.
> When it is let loose, it stays still.
> I have realized that, like a camel when bound or unbound, it
>   is paradoxical.

c. Highlighting the Key Points of the Method of Resting

This includes resting (1) like a Brahmin spinning thread, (2) like a straw bale after its rope is cut, (3) like a small child looking at a temple, and (4) like pricking an elephant with a thorn.

Resting like a Brahmin spinning thread

A thread requires a balance between tightness and looseness. Similarly, if the mind is too tight during meditation, it slips into thoughts, and if it is too loose, it remains dull. Therefore, tightness and looseness must be balanced.

Beginners should start by tightening up, abruptly slashing sudden thoughts. When this becomes irritating, they should let whatever arises be. Alternating as such, after a while tightness and looseness will naturally become balanced.[15]

With this in mind, it is taught to first constrict by tightening and then relax by loosening using the analogy known as "resting like a Brahmin spinning thread."

Resting like a straw bale after its rope is cut

All the preceding remedies consisted of merely thinking, "A thought has arisen, so I must not wander." The remedy arrives after the thought has ceased. Since this is all that has been happening, it is known as mindfulness that lags behind. It is a stain on meditation.

Abandon this type of mindful knowing[16] and just rest naturally in the continuity of shamatha. To rest the mind like this, free of activity and effort, is what is called "resting like a straw bale after its rope is cut."

Resting like a small child looking at a temple

Once the elephant of the mind is firmly tied to the pillar of mindful knowing the energies become stabilized in their original location. This causes all sorts of temporary experiences to occur. For instance, you may imagine empty forms, like smoke; you may experience such bliss that you feel about to faint; or you may be without thoughts, feeling as though you had neither body nor mind and were suspended in empty space.

No matter what experiences arise, do not be delighted and deliberately cling to them nor do anything to suppress them by regarding them as faults. In this way, you neither block nor cling to objects of perception. This is what is known as "resting like a small child looking at a temple."

Resting like pricking an elephant with a thorn

In the state of stillness, an emerging thought and the mindfulness that recognizes it arise at the same time. Thus, the undesirable and the antidote meet chest-to-chest; a thought cannot be followed by a second one. One does not need to apply the remedy with effort—it is automatic. For this reason, this mindfulness is called "mindfulness held by itself." When noticing that a thought has arisen, to neither engage in suppressing nor pursuing is what is meant by "resting like pricking an elephant with a thorn." This is the final stillness, called "like the ocean without waves."

At this point, on stillness, movement is recognized, and on movement the natural place of stillness is captured. Hence, this is known as the collapse of the division between stillness and movement, and it constitutes the realization of one-pointedness. Then that which recognizes stillness and movement is called right thinking, discerning knowledge, or self-cognizance. As it is said in the *Ornament of the Sutras (Sutralamkara)*:

Then, once his body and mind are thoroughly trained,
And he has attained the greatness of stable shamatha
He should know how to include discursive analysis.

B. Examining the Root of Stillness and Movement, Recognizing Vipashyana, and Meditating within the Yoga of Simplicity

This includes (1) examining the root of stillness and movement, (2) identifying vipashyana, and (3) cultivating the yoga of simplicity.

1. Examining the Root of Stillness and Movement

Regarding nonconceptual shamatha, which arises as discerning wisdom, investigate in the following way: When the mind rests still, what is the identity of this stillness like? How does it rest? How does movement occur from it? When there is movement, does it move after stillness has vanished? Or does it move while it is resting still? Is that movement something other than stillness or is it not? What is its identity like? Finally, how does the movement stop?

Since movement separate from stillness, or stillness separate from movement, cannot be established, there is no identity of stillness or movement to be found. At this point, examine the cognizance that observes these. Is it something other than the stillness or movement observed, or it is precisely that stillness or movement?

Through examining with the sight of your awareness, nothing whatsoever is found, and so you realize that observer and observed are inseparable. The identity of cognizance cannot be established as being anything. Therefore, this is known as the view transcending concepts, or the view that asserts nothing.[17] As Gyalwe Wangpo said:

> Even "good" conceptual views are destroyed.
> With no thoughts, even the term "view" does not exist.

The certainty that the observer and observed are inseparable
Is found through the kindness of the guru.

The teacher Shantideva refers precisely to this manner of investigation:

He who exerts himself in samadhi by all means,
Without straying for even an instant,
Investigates, "What is this mind of mine?"
In this way, he examines the mind in detail.

This also has been described through the example of wood and fire in the *Sutra Requested by Kashyapa* (*Kashyapa Parivarta Sutra*):

Through rubbing two pieces of wood, fire is produced,
Which in turn burns up the two pieces of wood.
Likewise, once the faculty of *prajna* emerges,
It burns up duality.[18]

This type of examination is carried out by self-knowing awareness, which focuses its observation inward. Therefore, it is called the analytical meditation of a simple practitioner. It is not the analytical meditation of a scholar, for the cognizance of a scholar is focused outward.

2. Identifying Vipashyana

No matter what arises, whether a thought or an affliction, neither reject it nor be carried away by it. Whatever arises, let it be. Through identifying it the very moment it is born and not rejecting it, it turns into its natural state of emptiness and manifests as such. In this manner, you can use all adversities as the path, and so this is called "taking adversities as the path."

Thoughts are liberated merely by recognizing them. Thus, you realize that what is to be abandoned and its remedy are inseparable.

This constitutes the heart of Vajrayana practice, known as "reversed meditation."[19]

Then, a superior compassion for all those beings who have not recognized the nature of their minds is born. For the sake of all beings, you then might spend all your time devoting body, speech, and mind to the path of means, such as the practices of the development stage. However, since that type of prajna has totally purified reifying fixation, these practices will not turn into delusion. It is like the taking of poison after it has been transformed by mantra recitation. Regarding this style of practice, it has been called "the path of neither adopting nor rejecting whatever arises."

3. Cultivating the Yoga of Simplicity

This includes (1) analyzing in terms of the three times, (2) analyzing in terms of substantiality or insubstantiality, and (3) analyzing in terms of singularity or multiplicity.

a. Analyzing in Terms of the Three Times

The mind of the past has ceased and is finished. The mind of the future has not been born, it has not yet arisen. There is nothing identifiable as the mind of the present. By investigating in this way, the nature of all phenomena is similarly destroyed. Reflect on this point and understand that every single phenomenon is unreal; phenomena are but mere designations of one's conceptual mind. Therefore, they are not born, do not abide, and do not cease. Examine it, as explained by Saraha:

> Once the notion of birth as something substantial
>   disappears like space
> And all substantiality is ruled out, what is there to be born?
> Everything is by nature primordially unborn.
> This has been shown today by the lord guru, and I have
>   realized it.

b. Analyzing in Terms of Substantiality or Insubstantiality

Is your mind existent and substantial? Or is it nonexistent and insubstantial? If it is substantial, is it found in the object or in the subject? If found in the object, what is its shape and color? Apply the same analysis to the subject. If the mind is nothing— insubstantial—what creates its various manifestations?

If an existing essence were found through investigation, it would be right to establish it as substantial. However, when one consciously investigates, nothing whatsoever is found to exist. Therefore, one cannot establish it as an existing, substantial thing. Since it is experienced by the wisdom of self-awareness, it also does not fall within the category of being nonexistent and insubstantial.

Therefore, it transcends both substantiality and insubstantiality, and so it neither falls into the path of eternalism nor nihilism. This is called the Middle Way, or Madhyamaka.

We did not understand this by means of the logician's system of following the signs back and forth. Rather, it was like seeing a treasure in the palm of one's hand through the pith instructions of the guru. On account of this, it is called great, or *maha*. As is said by Saraha:

> To take to heart what the guru has said,
> Is like seeing a treasure in the palm of one's hand.

c. Analyzing in Terms of Singularity or Multiplicity

Is this mind only one mind, or are there many minds? Let us suppose it is one. This mind is understood as various kinds of perceptions. Then how can it be one? If there are multiple minds, then how is it that all these perceptions become the same in regards to emptiness, which is their essence? Investigating in this way, finding that mind transcends both distinctions and freedom from extremes, is called the mahamudra of complete non-dwelling.

A yogin who has this realization, when resting in composure, experiences only the wisdom of self-knowing awareness. He experiences no other phenomenon at all apart from this, and so it is called the absence of phenomena. During post-meditation, all phenomena appear as illusory because the yogin has purified reification. As said by Saraha:

> In front, behind, and in the ten directions,
> Whatever I see is that itself.
> Today, the lord has severed delusions related to the ego.
> Now, I will ask no questions of anyone.

II. Special Practice

This includes (1) the yoga of one taste: all phenomena have the same taste in inseparable appearances and mind; and (2) the yoga of nonmeditation: one finally establishes that all phenomena are the innate co-emergent dharmakaya.

A. The Yoga of One Taste

This includes (1) pointing out appearances as mind through the analogy of sleep and dream, (2) pointing out the indivisibility of appearances and emptiness through the analogy of water and ice, and (3) establishing the same taste of all phenomena through the analogy of water and waves.

1. The Analogy of Sleep and Dream

No matter what you experience during sleep, no appearances are independent from your mind. Similarly, all present appearances are dreams occurring in the sleep of delusion. They do not exist apart from your mind. Therefore, whatever phenomena appear as an object, relax and rest right there. By doing just that, the outer object perceived and your mind will merge as one taste, inseparably and without duality. As the Lord of Yogins said:

> The dream you experienced last night
> Is the teacher who points out phenomena as the mind.
> Have you understood him?

And:

> Dye all these three worlds without exception
> With the color of great passion.

2. The Analogy of Water and Ice

No matter how phenomena appear, right at the time they manifest their essence cannot be found to exist. Therefore, they are said to be empty. But although they do not exist, they still appear in all kinds of ways. Thus, this is known as the indivisibility, or same taste, of appearances and emptiness like, for example, ice and water. The indivisibility of bliss and emptiness, clarity and emptiness, and awareness and emptiness should also be understood in the same way. Therefore, this is called the "realization of multiplicity as one taste." As it is said:

> Once you realize it, everything is that.
> No one can find anything separate from it.
> Reading, memorizing, and meditation are also the same.

3. The Analogy of Water and Waves

This is the realization that, just as waves arise from water itself, all phenomena are created through the essence of one's mind, emptiness arising as all phenomena. Saraha said:

> Since everything is projected by the mind,
> It is by nature the primordial lord.

A single absolute nature (dharmata) extends through the entire absolute space of phenomena (*dharmadhatu*), and this is known as "one taste arising as multiplicity." For a yogin who has realized this, the ensuing cognizance is that emptiness which extends to everything.

B. The Yoga of Nonmeditation

After finally establishing that all phenomena are the innate co-emergent dharmakaya, the yoga of nonmeditation is practiced. What was to be abandoned, the afflictive emotions, are exhausted, so the remedy that accomplished this abandonment is also exhausted, and the path comes to an end. There is nowhere else to go and nothing to begin. There is nothing higher than this to build up to. One attains the supreme siddhi of Mahamudra, the non-dwelling nirvana. As is said in the main text of the teaching cycle on integrating:

> *Kye ho!* This wisdom of self-awareness
> Transcends words and is not experienced by conceptual
>   mind.
> I, Tilopa, have nothing whatsoever to reveal.
> Point it out to yourself and know it!

Also,

> Do not recall, don't imagine, do not examine,
> Do not meditate, do not think;
> Rest in the natural flow.

CONCLUSION

This section includes (1) identifying mahamudra and pointing out one's nature, (2) examining obstacles and strayings, and (3) distinguishing between temporary experience, realization, and intellectual understanding.

I. Identifying Mahamudra and Pointing Out One's Nature

This includes (1) establishing the ground, (2) practicing the path, (3) making fine distinctions between experiences, (4) distinguishing the signs of progress of the bhumis and the paths, and (5) actualizing the fruit. All these are dealt with in the four yogas.

II. Examining Obstacles and Types of Straying
A. The Three Obstacles

1. The obstacle of phenomena arising as enemies: this is removed by knowing that phenomena are mind.
2. The obstacle of thoughts arising as enemies: this is removed by knowing that thoughts are the dharmakaya.
3. The obstacle of emptiness arising as an enemy: this is removed by knowing that phenomena and emptiness are indivisible.

B. The Three Deviations

These consist of clinging to the experiences of shamatha. They are removed by progressing in the practice of vipashyana.

C. The Four Types of Straying

1. Misunderstanding emptiness as being a concrete nature: this is stopped by allowing emptiness to arise as compassion.
2. Straying into labeling: this is stopped by realizing the true mode of being as it is.
3. Straying into remedies: this is stopped by realizing that the remedy and what is to be abandoned are inseparable.
4. Straying onto a path: this is stopped by realizing that arising and liberation are simultaneous.

III. Distinguishing Between Temporary Experience, Realization, and Intellectual Understanding

To understand the natural state of the mind through learning and contemplation is intellectual understanding. A one-pointed understanding in the manner of a mental image is temporary experience. The direct understanding that takes place during the yoga of simplicity and the other higher yogas is realization. Although all three are commonly called understanding, there is no conflict.

Shenpen Zangpo, the king of Kashmir and Zangskar, told me he needed a text of notes on mahamudra and the six yogas of Naropa. He asked me to write these and made a special offering of a measure of saffron pistil. I have written this only to benefit future generations, without consulting any of my numerous relevant notes on the teachings of the oral transmission. It was composed while I was staying at Kharchu Changchub Nyingpo in the South.

May there be goodness!

The Six Cycles of Equal Taste in a Nutshell

Pema Karpo

I prostrate to all the sublime gurus!

Remaining in undistracted samadhi in forests and caves,
With the lion's strength of dignity of supreme wisdom,
Teaching those with elephantine materialistic fixations,
I prostrate at the feet of the glorious Drukpa.

Here is a threefold discussion of the six cycles of equal taste corresponding to the path of liberation, summing up equal taste into Mahamudra. This includes (1) the history of the lineage, and (2) the instructions.

THE HISTORY OF THE LINEAGE

This is similar to the supplication to the lineage gurus.

THE INSTRUCTIONS

This includes (1) the introduction and (2) the actual practice.

I. The Introduction

Think to yourself, "Once I have released all beings from the prison of samsara I will establish them within unsurpassable enlightenment. For this purpose, I will practice this profound teaching of

the equal taste of whatever occurs until actualizing its profundity."
Rest your body at ease. See yourself as Vajrayogini. On the crown
of your head visualize the lineage gurus one on top of the other.
Recite the equal taste supplication. Finally, the gurus melt into
light and dissolve into yourself. Then, turning away from the mind
moving toward objects, rest in the continuity of the mind as it is.

II. The Actual Practice

This has six cycles.

A. Instructions on Using Thoughts as the Path

Taking bad omens as good fortune includes (1) the introduction,
which is to establish the determination; (2) the main practice,
which is to rest in emptiness; and (3) the conclusion, which is to
equalize the taste.

1. Setting Up the Determination

Since thoughts are the primary source for being cast into samsara,
we do not want them to arise and reject them when they do. Here,
unless you know how to use them, you will not be able to traverse
them as the path because you will consider thoughts as something
to be eliminated with a remedy. Therefore, revert from what is ordinary and practice reverse meditation. Equalize sights, sounds, and
cognitions as occurring evenly within self-knowing awareness. In
this regard, no matter how numerous thoughts may be, the strength
of wisdom will be enhanced to the same extent, like fire encounter-
ing fuel. Hence, when a thought arises there should only be joy.

2. Resting in Emptiness

When a thought arises, if its essence is recognized right there, by
that alone it will be liberated upon arising. Having reverted from

ignorance, that is the wisdom of awareness. If not recognized, that becomes ignorance itself. In the first case, the thought itself is labeled as a remedy, and there is no other remedy apart from that. This being the case, discarding and applying the remedy are inseparable, samsara and nirvana are the same, and thoughts are the dharmakaya. At that time, this recognition happens because one is able to maintain the direct continuity of awareness or mind, otherwise it is not experienced. Therefore, in the *Prediction of the Wisdom Mind Tantra (Sandhi Vyakarana Tantra)* it is said:

> The first mind is shamatha;
> Seeing repeatedly immobility and so forth
> Is called vipashyana.

What is taught here is shamatha and vipashyana in union. This is the root of the practice in a nutshell.

3. Equalizing the Taste

Thus, since the recognized object and the cognizance that recognizes it are not two, there is sameness, like water poured into water. When no thought occurs, you remain undistracted without modifying. When a thought occurs, recognize it the very moment it arises without allowing it to be followed by a second one.

B. Using Afflictive Emotions as the Path

Turning poison into nectar also has three parts.

1. Setting Up the Determination

Think in this special way: Let afflictions arise! Stir them! Be carried away by them!

2. Resting in Emptiness

If we condense the main and secondary afflictions, they come down to five. Regarding the afflictions that are akin to delusion, at the time of sleep, by focusing undistractedly directly on sleep, the dissolution stages of sleep are self-liberated. The practice consists of recognizing the ground luminosity. For that, rest the mind on what you have been previously familiarized with. As it is said, "Enter the luminosity."

Regarding the afflictions that are akin to attachment, there are ten types of passion, the final being fainting into ecstasy. When one recognizes the essence of passion, there is no fainting; that is precisely what is called the great bliss of self-knowing awareness.

Regarding the afflictions that are akin to aggression, if at the time of anger its essence is recognized, lucidity increases. This will be able to free and guide during wrathful conduct and the like. As is illustrated by these points, proceed in the same way for pride and jealousy.

3. Equalizing the Taste

Thus, since an affliction is simply empty of itself, it is self-liberated, so it is said that the affliction is wisdom.

C. Instructions on Using Gods and Demons as the Path

Reducing obstacles to the siddhis has three parts.

1. Setting Up the Determination

Whether one goes to an isolated mountain retreat, a place of secret conduct, or in brief anywhere that is terrifying, if one does not feel the apprehension that an obstacle may arise, establish a joyful determination, for obstacles are the guides to siddhis.

2. Resting in Emptiness

While in these places, when an apparition of a magical creation of gods or demons arises, if you feel afraid, is it the body or the mind that is afraid? If it is the body, visualize it as a ransom for beings and give it away to gods and demons. Since the mind is emptiness no one is able to harm it. If you continue to be afraid, since it is oneself who has created that which is being afraid, through examination of the essence of the creator, it becomes self-liberated. Fear becomes the inspiration for spiritual practice.

3. Equalizing the Taste

If gods and demons are seen as such, that faulty vision brings about obstacles to one's life and lifespan. When fixation on gods and demons is recognized, the maras arise as Dharma protectors and obstacles become siddhis.

D. Using Suffering As the Path

This instruction on bodhichitta has three parts.

1. Setting Up the Determination

Do not regard suffering as a fault; consider that if you are wandering in samsara suffering happens and that's the way it is. This is a consequence of negative conduct in previous lives coming to fruition at this time. Since now that negativity is extinguished, think that this is something to rejoice in. Therefore, if it happens, be glad.

2. Resting in Emptiness

This includes (1) mind training on relative bodhichitta and (2) mind training on absolute bodhichitta.

Mind training on relative bodhichitta

Any suffering that may arise, physical or other, is similar to the various sufferings afflicting all beings. Therefore, condense the sufferings of all beings into this one, and wish that they all find happiness. Think that for as long as all of them are in need of your concern, you will be responsible.

Mind training on absolute bodhichitta

If you are suffering, look at the essence of that suffering. That suffering has never existed, and due to this key point there is no other way but for it to be self-purified. There is no happiness other than being free from suffering. Therefore this is called using suffering as happiness.

3. Equalizing the Taste

Suffering thus becomes the bodhichitta practice of exchanging oneself for others and ultimately becomes the best method for training on the path.

E. Using Sickness as the Path

The instruction on equalizing the taste of the elements has three parts.

1. Setting Up the Determination

Since sickness is the "broom" of accomplishment, adversity is a spiritual friend and pain is the purifier of obscurations. If they occur, be joyful.

2. Resting in Emptiness

When you are sick, do not indulge in an attitude of rejection, but think, "May all the illnesses afflicting beings similar to this sickness be absorbed into it! May they be happy! For as long as all of them are in need of my concern, I will be responsible!" This is the reverse meditation of compassion.

Then by analyzing sickness, pain, and the one who is sick, it is impossible to apprehend them; they cannot be established as anything whatsoever. Rest there without movement. This is called emptiness's reverse meditation.

If again sickness arises, practice alternatively compassion's reverse meditation and emptiness's reverse meditation as before.

3. Equalizing the Taste

Since the cause of this suffering is the afflicting emotions, this is resolved by using afflictions as the path. Since the conditions are conceptual thought, by using thoughts, afflictions, and gods and demons as the path, conditions are cleared. The resultant sickness being suffering, by developing the potential of the two kinds of equal taste, sickness is defeated. Tokden Gonye said:

> From almost collapsing and dying thirteen times,
> The yogi finds the great confidence of knowing.
> This precious kind adversity
> Is unmatched by the hundreds of favorable conditions.

F. Using Death as the Path

The instruction on pointing out the mother and child has three parts.

1. Setting Up the Determination

If you know you are going to die, do not regard it as a shortcoming, but think that through dying you will actualize the dharmakaya.

2. Resting in Emptiness

This consists of using subtle and coarse death. Subtle death is the instantaneous birth and cessation: a past instance has ceased, that itself is death, and the next instance is birth. So, if you recognize any arising thought, right at that interval moment the mother luminosity appears. Recognizing this is the meeting of the mother and child. Jetsun (Milarepa) said:

> Taste the flow of primordial wisdom that arises
> In the interval between past and future thoughts.

Coarse death is the termination of life; at the end of the stages of dissolution outer breath ceases, while at the fourth instant of the inner breath, luminosity arises. Identifying the dissolution stages, they are purified, whereby ground luminosity is recognized. This purifies all habitual tendencies, through which one awakens to Buddhahood.

3. Equalizing the Taste

Since the luminosity at the moment of death has been identified, death is no longer apprehended conceptually. This leads you to attain the deathless innate truth.

The instruction on the sixfold cycle has thus been presented. When practicing them, merge your mind with the guru's and maintain meditative composure. At that time, from thoughts to death, these do not arise in that order. Since you develop the potential whenever you encounter any of these situations, this is called the single-session practice.

This advice given in a nutshell was written by the bhikshu Pema Karpo in response to the constant and persistent request by a dignitary in the Gyaltse Luwang Garden.

DISTINGUISHING THE FOUR YOGAS WITH CERTAINTY

The Unsurpassed Among All Mahamudra Explanations

PEMA KARPO

Homage to the precious Kagyu!

In the center of the basic space of E is VAṂ.
I bow at the feet of the glorious guru
who always plays with delight
in the sublime and secret definitive meaning.

The ground, experience in practice, signs of heat, and the fruition, indeed the whole path is condensed into the four yogas, which are to be directly actualized. Experience comes from practicing the path, which accords with how the ground is resolved; there is a connection between how that path is traversed and how it manifests.

In order to be stainless, to not reside anywhere, to be without contradiction, and to be free of a reference point, the four yogas of one-pointedness, simplicity, one taste, and nonmeditation are taught. All phenomena that are known to be thoroughly afflicted and their complete purification are clarified and presented here. Because they do not exist in the slightest way, phenomena are stainless.

There is no reality at all that can be ascribed to the two categories of existence and nonexistence. Not fixating on the middle either, reality is said not to reside anywhere. Among all phenomena that can be found, none are apart from this. Because suchness also permeates all aspects of everything, it is without any contradiction. Even the omniscient ones don't have the words to fully express this. It is not an object of the intellect and cannot be grasped by example. Therefore, it is free of reference point.

Through the nonconceptual, the unborn, the nondual, and the inconceivable, one may come to rest in the natural state. There are thus four ways of practicing the path. However much one grasps things as being real is how much one is trapped in the prison of existence. Therefore, completely cast away fixation on reality and also do not conceptualize the unreal.

> Where do things come from? Where do they abide? Where
>   do they cease?
> Not finding anything is the suchness without root, the
>   settling in the unborn.

No matter how many thoughts proliferate, all are the nature of the mind itself. So, rest evenly in the nonduality of existence and emptiness. Because there is not even the slightest meditation, there is also nothing to meditate on. Beyond meditating and meditation objects, there is an inconceivable awareness. Fine distinctions are proclaimed between the experiences of the four yogas of one-pointedness, simplicity, one taste, and nonmeditation:

> When the nature of movement is known in the midst of
>   stillness,
> And one settles naturally in stillness in the midst of
>   movement,
> The division between stillness and movement falls away.
> This is the recognition of one-pointedness.

Simplicity is the complete pacification of the designations of arising and ceasing, permanence and nothingness, coming and going, and oneness and multiplicity. It is also a realization that is not simply a thoughtless absence.

One taste is properly realizing that the nature of all things is the very essence of one's own mind. Through this, one sees that everything is this way and nothing is ever otherwise.

The yoga of nonmeditation is the exhaustion of all phenomena in basic space, in which what is to be discarded and their remedies are simultaneously exhausted, like fire and its fuel.

The specific individual capacities of practitioners are categorized as those who are instantaneous, those who crossover in leaps, and those who are gradual. Because there are these three types of individuals, it is explained that realization unfolds in three different ways. There are also lesser, middling, and greater levels of each yoga related to not attaining stability, attaining stability, or attaining complete stability, respectively. Thus, there are twelve total divisions taught.

The four yogas explained in this way each have four associated qualities, and so there are sixteen divisions as well:

Seeing the essence, thoughts arise as meditation;
Perfecting one's capacity, qualities arise;
Understanding the nature of relative appearances
Determines whether one plants the seed of the
  nirmanakaya.

Those who see the ultimate have proclaimed that one-pointedness correlates with the path of joining and simplicity with the path of seeing; one taste relates to the path of meditation and nonmeditation to the path of no more learning. For example, just as the path of joining has twelve subdivisions, so too does one-pointedness.

Through these four uncommon divisions, the four yogas are condensed. The perfect buddhas have extensively taught the four divisions of not accomplishing and the three stages of lesser, middling, and greater accomplishment.

To never waver from the dharmakaya is one-pointedness. That itself, completely free from all obscurations, is simplicity. From that state, to display the activity of benefitting others is one taste.

That, moreover, is without beginning or end, and so is taught as nonmeditation.

This expresses the four yogas whose results have been actualized. I have here conveyed a little bit of the extremely profound meaning of what I received from the kindness of the sublime guru. Please forgive any faults there may be.

———————

This was arranged in Mokpa Lhatse Monastery, a great sacred place that has been blessed by the best among the accomplished ones.

May it be virtuous!

Maṅgalam!

POINTING OUT THE SUBLIME ESSENTIAL MEANING

An Explanation of the Four Yogas

PEMA KARPO

Homage to the noble Lord of Speech! [20]

To those who have experience in the definitive meaning, and yet are poor in its mere expression, I offer the following explanation.

When the nature of movement is known in the midst of stillness,
And one settles naturally in stillness in the midst of movement,
The division between stillness and movement falls away.
This is the recognition of one-pointedness.

When the confidence of freedom is found in the midst of
    confusion,
And the hidden flaw of confusion is known within freedom,
The division between confusion and freedom falls away.
This is the recognition of simplicity.

When the innate nature of mind is known in the midst of
    appearances,
And the way appearances arise is realized within mind,
The division between appearances and mind falls away.
This is the recognition of one taste.

When one does not waver from the flow of suchness in
   post-meditation,
And compassion spontaneously overflows in meditative
   composure,
The division between meditation and post-meditation falls away.
This is the recognition of nonmeditation.

1. One-Pointedness

Within the undistracted aspect of stability, as soon as the slightest
movement stirs, allow it to naturally vanish on its own. Knowing
the slightest stirring of movement within the aspect of stability
is known as "recognizing the nature of movement in the midst of
stillness."

As soon as there is the slightest stirring, before it continues from
the first thought to the second, to come to rest in stillness is known
as "naturally settling in stillness in the midst of movement." At this
stage, knowing the slightest stirring and being free of movement
happen at the same time. It is not the case that while there is stability, there is movement on top of that, because movement occurs
due to a slight inability to remain in stillness. Instead, due to the
qualities of settling in stillness, this is recognized right away and
one returns to stillness. On this matter, some say it is like the fish
of insight swimming in the vast ocean of calm abiding.

At that time, the knowing of arising is also a quality of stillness.
The knower of that is called awareness or discriminating awareness.[21] Therefore, through analysis in the context of nonreferential
calm abiding, authentic insight arises. From *Entering the Way of
the Bodhisattva* (*Bodhicharyavatara*):

> This mind of mine, a wild and rampant elephant,
> I will tether to that sturdy post, reflection upon the teaching,
> And I shall narrowly stand guard
> So that it might never slip its bonds and flee.

> Those who strive to master concentration
> Should never for an instant be distracted.
> They should constantly investigate themselves,
> Examining the movement of their minds.[22]

Furthermore, the precious Kagyu masters have taught:

> Blankness without movement of thoughts and lacking the
>   clarity aspect
> Is a neutral state of thoughtless vacancy.

It is taught that those who maintain that state, mistaking it for calm abiding, will be reborn as animals. This agrees with Jetsun Sakya Pandita's remark:

> If fools engage in Mahamudra meditation, this will mostly become a cause for animal birth.

What then distinguishes calm abiding from that state? Calm abiding is imbued with the experiences of bliss, clarity, and no thoughts. Furthermore, being undistracted, there is a knowing of subtle sensations, even down to the mere vibration of a hair. Thoughtless vacancy does not include any of these qualities!

By saying that "bliss, clarity, and no thoughts are the potential pitfalls of meditation," what is meant is that calm abiding experiences of bliss, clarity, and no thoughts, as ends in themselves, are sidetracks into the three realms of existence. Thus it is also said:

> If not that, then they are born into the formless realm.

In that kind of calm abiding, that which makes activity in meditation dissolve into space; this is called dull calm abiding. A single absorption can last weeks at a time. By meditating like that, an eon may pass and it will become the absorption of cessation. It was said:

Or else, they fall into the cessation of the hearers.

At that time, it is taught that one must destroy the meditation. The Dharma lord Tsangpa Gyare said:

Many know how to meditate, but few know how to destroy meditation!

Barawa also said:

Meditators will be deceived by meditation.

Even after destroying meditation, one should then progress into simplicity, relying on the instructions. Even if one has meditated well on calm abiding, it is said that "there is nothing superior to meditating on the Middle Way."

Considering that analyzing merely in this way does not transcend the Sutra path, the precious Kagyu teaches, "Strive in devotion, the enhancement of meditation!" This and similar crucial points are greatly cherished. This agrees completely with Gyalwang Je:

One can doubt whether liberation will come through endurance in meditation, but there is no doubt that one can be liberated through devotion. It is the difference between grasping and not grasping the crucial point!

If one does not understand this key point and simply proclaims that the preceding argument is a refutation of Mahamudra, this is a fault of not having investigated the subtle distinctions of the path of calm abiding. It is taught that the point of the yoga of calm abiding is to improve over and over again until finally reaching the nine states of meditative absorption. But here, because the advancement to simplicity only comes from this particular type of one-pointedness, one does not rely on attaining the nine absorptions. How could this not be so? As Lopön Pawo said:

> Beings who go astray from your [the Buddha's] teachings,
> blinded by ignorance, may have reached the summit of
> worldly existence,[23] but suffering will arise again and
> existence will persist. Followers of your teachings, even if
> they do not attain the main body of meditative concen-
> tration, will be untouched by maras, and samsara will be
> purified and averted, left behind like a pile of grass.

It is indeed taught that insight can arise without relying on the
main practice of meditative concentration.

Some so-called scholars whose view of the ultimate has become
blinded assert:

> There will be no realization of authentic emptiness
> without prior analysis through scripture and reason-
> ing. Therefore, one should first engage in the profound
> analysis of scripture and reasoning.

However, from the *Condensed Hevajra Tantra*:

> Because it is a sequence of blessings, the omniscient pri-
> mal wisdom is just like that.

It is also said:

> No one else can express the innate, and it cannot be found
> anywhere. It will be known through being pointed out
> by the guru and one's own merit.

This primarily explains that realization occurs due to the blessings of the sublime guru. In most scriptures of the Unsurpassable
Tantra class, it is only taught that realization arises by the power
of wind-energy (*prana*) and the mind entering the central channel.
The explanation that analysis of scripture and reasoning yields realization is nowhere to be found. Even in the Sutra path it is taught

that the truth can be seen by merely being struck by the Tathagata's light rays. Also, there are examples such as the bodhisattva Sadpra-rudita seeing truth through unwavering devotion to the buddha Dharmodgata, truth being seen through simply applying the mind to the Prajnaparamita, Shariputra seeing it through hearing a verse recited once, and so forth.

Furthermore, except for in calm abiding, all investigation only serves to promote conceptuality. Thus, all those who are skilled in the key points of the relative and ultimate truths unanimously assert that nonconceptuality is not determined through concepts.

So, with the perspective that one must first give rise to nonreferential calm abiding in order to investigate with discriminating wisdom, the cause of the arising of insight, Shantideva declared:

> Having understood that insight, which fully incorporates
>   calm abiding,
> Completely vanquishes afflictions,
> Calm abiding is the first objective to be sought.

Also, it is taught in *Entering the Middle Way* (*Madhyamakavatara*):

> Ordinary beings are bound by concepts. Nonconcep-
> tual yogins will be free.

From the textual tradition of the fearless Chandrakirti:

> The teaching that asserts analyzing through scripture
> and reasoning comes first is also only for the sake of
> giving rise to nonconceptual and nonreferential calm
> abiding. The victors have taught that the reversal of con-
> ceptual grasping is the fruition of investigation.

If one thinks that scripture and reasoning serve no purpose in giv-ing rise to nonreferential calm abiding, this is also not the case. From *Entering the Middle Way*:

> The buddhas have taught that without objects to be known, the knower is easily dispensed with. Because the knower is disproved if there are no objects to be known, the objects of knowledge are the first to be refuted.

With the perspective that the knower is easily refuted if the objects of knowing are negated, one first examines by way of scripture and reasoning, and then from that point on, one strives for nonreferential calm abiding. In order for the mind to rest in a state of no contrivance, one has to train with great fortitude. From the *King of Samadhi Sutra* (*Samadhiraja Sutra*):

> The learned ones, having understood the conditioned and the unconditioned, completely vanquish all perceptions of characteristics. While resting in the absence of characteristics, they fully comprehend the emptiness of all things.

Also, in Jowo Atisha's *Lamp of the Path of Awakening* (*Bodhipathapradipa*):

> Through scripture and reasoning, one will gain confidence that all phenomena, having an unborn nature, do not really exist. Thus, one should meditate on nonconceptuality. Meditating on suchness in that way, one will progressively accomplish the stages of heat and so forth, and then attain the level of Great Joy on up, and the Buddha's awakening will not take long to reach.

And:

> If the branches of calm abiding become weak, even if one meditates with great exertion for thousands of years, one will still not accomplish samadhi.

Therefore, reflect and see for yourself whether this assertion that realization of emptiness can only come through the investigation of scripture and reasoning is confused about the definitive meaning.

It is also not the case that calm abiding taught from the Middle Way tradition must necessarily be preceded by investigation with scripture and reasoning. In *Entering the Way of the Bodhisattva*:

> Moreover, those who are unattached to the world will achieve the realm of True Joy.

Furthermore:

> Compared to wishing for insight from practicing calm abiding with attributes, this path (of nonreferential calm abiding) is much more profound.

In Lopön Bodhibhadra's *Chapter on the Collected Verses of Samadhi* (*Samadhi Sambhara Parivarta*):

> Therefore, compared to relying on calm abiding with attributes, it is considered better to give rise to insight having focused on nonreferential calm abiding. By remaining steadfast in this approach, through nonreferential calm abiding alone, afflictions will completely cease and be cleared away because it is a cause in harmony with the result.

Realization of authentic insight comes through investigation by means of discriminating wisdom and nonreferential calm abiding. At that time, however, that insight purifies or destroys those two. In Lopön Bodhibhadra's words:

> One might ask if it is acceptable to give rise to insight without engaging in calm abiding with attributes beforehand. It is acceptable. From discriminating wisdom and

nonreferential calm abiding comes nonconceptual wakefulness, insight without characteristics.

This is also taught in the *Sutra Requested by Noble Kashyapa*:

Fire arises from rubbing two sticks together, which then
burns the two sticks. Similarly, suchness arises from
conceptual wisdom and sense faculties, and that suchness burns those two.

This being the case, there is also the so-called unity of experience
and realization. How is it that the experiences of bliss, clarity, and
no thoughts arising from nonreferential calm abiding are in unity
with the realization of insight? One has realization that the nature
of the object is emptiness. One has the experience that the nature
of the subject is luminosity. In this way, they are expressed as the
union of experience and realization.

It is often said that bliss, clarity, and no thoughts are the highest
summit of meditation. However, only by defining bliss as unchanging supreme bliss, clarity as the luminous nature, and no thoughts
as emptiness can these be asserted as the summit of meditation.
This has been expressed in this way in order to steadily abide until
reaching the level of Buddhahood.

The insight that is taught in the context of the unity of calm
abiding and insight is merely the general meaning of insight. Likewise, the calm abiding from the unity of calm abiding and insight
is not the calm abiding that is referred to here. Resting in the basic
space in which elaborations are pacified is calm abiding. Its radiance, the aspect of vivid awareness, is insight. This presentation is
the meaning of the unity of calm abiding and insight. As it is said:

First, the mind is to abide in calm, remain unwavering and
    so forth. . . .
Seeing with discernment is said to be insight.

Furthermore, not only in the texts of Chandrakirti, but also by the glorious Dharmakirti:

> Without disproving the object, one will be unable to abandon grasping to it.

By considering that it will be easy to destroy the true existence of the subject once the object is resolved as unreal, first one determines the object lacks reality. As it is taught in the *Condensed Prajnaparamita Sutra*:

> It is well known that the Buddha declared that perceptions belong to this shore. Having totally destroyed perceptions, one abandons them, and goes to the other shore.

In the words of Master Shantideva:

> The ways we merely see, hear, and know are not the objects of refutation. Taking things as real, the cause of suffering, is to be overturned.

Through determining that the subject—the knower—is unreal, the object will be naturally determined to lack any reality. Understanding this, one first sees the knower is not real. As it is said:

> Having completely cast away the mind and its objects,
> Relax loosely like a small child at rest.
> If you exert yourself with devotion, focusing on the oral
>   instructions of the guru,
> There is no doubt the innate will manifest.[24]

Also, Tilopa said:

> *Kye ho!* This self-aware original wakefulness is beyond the
>   way of words.

It is not in the domain of conceptual mind.
I, Tilopa, have nothing to show at all.
Understand that you must indicate it for yourself.

This approach is in complete harmony with the traditions of the great Saraha and the great seers Tilopa and Naropa. As it is said:

Without analyzing beforehand with scripture and reasoning, by meditating on the yoga of calm abiding, the tendency to perceive substantiality is abandoned. By meditating on the activity of discriminating wisdom, the tendency of calm abiding in emptiness is abandoned. It is taught that then the authentic realization of complete pacification arises.

As Shantideva said:[25]

Through cultivating a propensity for emptiness, the habit of perceiving substantiality is abandoned. By meditating on "nothing whatsoever," the view of emptiness also will fade away.

When "there is nothing" is proclaimed, one does not fixate on a substantial thing to be examined. At that time, how can an insubstantial and unsupported nonthing remain before the mind?

When both substantiality and insubstantiality are not beheld by the mind, there are no other options left. And so there is complete peace, free of any reference point.

However, in the context of the path of Mantra, the positions of these masters become aligned. As for that, objects of knowing are purely labels of the knowing mind. Apart from that, they merely appear as real by the power of fixation on their solidity. Therefore, until one determines that the knowing mind lacks any reality, even if the nonexistence of the known object is seen in countless ways, it will be impossible to destroy clinging to the reality of the known object. Therefore, this tradition of ours is a good one!

In this snowy land (Tibet), the distinction between analytic and resting meditation is as follows: the difference is whether analysis by way of scripture and reasoning is carried out beforehand. Even those who teach analytic meditation in the way of prior analysis also end up with resting meditation, because they too must settle the mind without contrivance. An example from the pith instructions of the Middle Way of Jowo Je Atisha:

> Do not conceptualize a knower whatsoever. Do not cling to anything at all. Abandon all thinking and mental engagement.

These days some consider the equipoise of leaving the mind uncontrived to be an enemy! They sit there teaching a view, thinking, "By engaging in our profound stages of meditation, there is emptiness, selflessness, and lack of reality!" By carrying on like that, however, it will be impossible to traverse the path of the noble ones. From the *Explanation of the Mind of Awakening* (*Bodhichittavivarana*) by the noble Nagarjuna:

> Whatever inferior meditation on "emptiness," whether it is called "non-arising," "empty," or "selfless," is in fact meditation on the self.

As is explained here, this is a distorted path. From the *Condensed Prajnaparamita Sutra*,

> Even if he thinks, "This aggregate is empty," the bodhisattva is engaging in characteristics, and is not faithful to the unborn state.

Emptiness is taught in order to discard the tendency to cling to substantiality. If it becomes one's view, however, it is like medicine that has turned into poison. You will not get to emptiness through having that sort of conceptual reference point in your mind! Lopön Pagpa taught:

> All virtuous and nonvirtuous thoughts have the characteristic of ceasing. Thus, the buddhas teach emptiness. Otherwise, "empty" should not be posited.

However, in your pith instructions, because there are ways of analyzing in terms of the three times, in terms of entities and non-entities, in terms of sameness and difference, and so forth, one might think that in the end the practice comes down to analytic meditation. But this is not the case. The analysis of analytic meditation evaluates by way of the logic of scripture and reasoning.

In this tradition of ours, by contrast, only on top of an undistracted stability of mind does an investigation through discriminating wisdom take place. Therefore, it does not stray even slightly from the meaning of resting meditation. This manner of investigation was taught by the great Saraha:

> In that way, while definitely not getting confused,
> One should know the true nature for oneself with certainty.
> It is not material, not immaterial, and it is also not mind.
> It is free of grasping to those concepts from the beginning.
> Saraha has not much more to say than that!

And:

> Where do things originate? Where do they cease? Where do they remain? These we cannot know.

And:

The notion of things really arising is completely pacified, like space. If things are abandoned, how will they
then arise again? From the beginning, their nature is
unborn. Through the teachings of the guru protector,
realize this today!

As for calm abiding, because it has the characteristic of a one-
pointed mind, it is called the yoga of one-pointedness. Some, thinking, "This yoga of one-pointedness is not clearly explained. . . ."
dispute even the term. But others have also not left the matter
unexplained. The glorious Jnanakirti said:

Furthermore, when authentic calm abiding of one-
pointedness has arisen . . .

Also, as the genuine and perfect Buddha himself declared in the
King of Samadhi Sutra:

If one asks, "What contentment comes from the essence
of samadhi?" one should see it like this: it leads to fully
accomplishing all manner of bliss, joyful happiness,
and one-pointedness. Also, if one asks, "What is the
presentation of samadhi?" one should see it like this: it
is one-pointedness, which results in becoming expert
in the nonorigination and nondestruction of mind and
mental factors.

This is a clear explanation of calm abiding as one-pointedness.

2. Simplicity

When the confidence of freedom is found in the midst of
confusion,
And the hidden flaw of confusion is known in the midst of
freedom,

The division between freedom and confusion falls away.
This is the recognition of simplicity.

In the midst of whatever confusion that arises, knowing it as groundless and rootless is called "finding the confidence of freedom in the midst of confusion." From that understanding of groundlessness and rootlessness, never finding any confused phenomena from then on is called "knowing the hidden flaw of confusion in the midst of freedom." Saraha said:

> Whoever gives attention to the suchness that has no basis—
> That is the best of the guru's instructions.
> The nature of samsara is the essence of mind.
> O confused ones . . . understand what Saraha is saying!

Also, from the *Sutra Requested by Gaganaganja* (*Gaganaganja Paripircha Sutra*):

> Son of noble family, look at how profound dependent origination is! Whatever results arise from causes do not veer from becoming results. Also, results do not arise without a cause. In this way, the profound nature of results arising from causes and conditions has its own reality. These two (causal efficacy and nothing arising without a cause) are unfailing and unproduced by anyone. Whoever perceives in this way is liberated. Why is this the case? The Victorious One also understood affliction, and the complete purification of that.

Purification does not come about through the clearing away of affliction. Rather, the characteristic of the very essence of affliction is complete purification. As it is said:

> What is known as thorough affliction and complete purification are just symbolic terms.

From the *Sutra That Teaches All Phenomena Are Unarisen* (*Sarvadharma Apravritti Nirdesha Sutra*):

> The Venerable One said, "How is it that you comprehend desire?"
> The householder's son replied, "Desire is understood as affliction."
> The Venerable One said, "But is that desire to be found inside or outside the mind?
> He replied, "Desire is not inside the mind. It is also not outside of it."
> The Venerable One then said, "Thus, if desire is not inside or outside, then it is also not in the east, in the south, in the west, nor in the north. It is not above, not below, and not in-between. Because it is indeed this way, it is unarisen. How could that which is unarisen be afflicted or purified?"

The great master Saraha, the accomplisher of suchness, said:

> In front, behind, and in all the ten directions,
> Whatever is seen is suchness.
> Today, I the protector have cut through all illusion.
> From now on, no need to ask questions to anyone!

In this way, it has been clearly expounded. By directly realizing the true nature of all phenomena, not merely understanding through abstract notions, all doubts are naturally destroyed. Therefore, it is known as cutting all reification from within. For example, it is similar to a person who is frightened due to mistaking a piece of rope for a snake. As soon as they come to know it is a rope, grasping to the idea of a snake will lose all basis and thereafter no characteristics of a snake whatsoever can be found in the rope.

Furthermore, because confusion—all afflictive phenomena—is not actually encountered anywhere, confusion is realized as groundless, and this is known as realizing the actual nature of confusion. If confusion does not exist, how could there be anything that is free from it? There is no such thing, and so the phenomenon of nirvana is nowhere to be found. Therefore, the nature is free of any establishing of confusion and freedom, or samsara and nirvana. Exactly that is called realizing all phenomena are empty and selfless. Not seeing anything is also referred to as the supreme seeing. From *Entering the Two Truths (Satyadvaya Avatara)* by Atisha:

> The way in which the ultimate is undivided
> Is that there are neither phenomenal entities nor any
>   intrinsic nature.

> Within emptiness, there is not the slightest bit of difference.
> As realization occurs in a nonconceptual way,
> "Seeing emptiness" is used as a convention.

> The extremely profound sutras teach that
> The not-seeing itself is actually "seeing."

In that way, the true nature of all phenomena, from form to complete omniscience, is not inherently existent, and thus is not "non-empty." "Empty" is also posited on the basis of "non-empty," and so because the "non-empty" is not existent in any way whatsoever, emptiness is likewise not established in the slightest way. Consequently, the inability to establish anything at all is called "being free of views and assertions." Furthermore, from the *Root Verses of the Middle Way (Mulamadhyamaka Karika)*:

> If the "non-empty" existed in the slightest way,
> The "empty" would also exist in the same slight way.

> If however there is not even the slightest non-empty thing,
> How could there be anything that is empty?

The conquerors taught emptiness in order to cast away all
  views.
It is proclaimed that accomplishment will be impossible
For those who turn emptiness into a view.

As for realizing that, from the *Treasury of Dohas* (*Doha Kosha*):

To keep in the heart whatever the guru teaches
Is like seeing a treasure placed in the palm of one's hand.

As for that, it is the introduction to the "ordinary mind." Toward
that which is known as the ordinary mind, these days many who
lack understanding think it is a bad thing. This is a big mistake;
they have not even understood the etymology of the term! *Prakrita*
is rendered as "nature" or "ordinary." Thus, the meaning is "natural
mind." If you think there is no authentic transmission of the meaning of the term, consider the great Lopön Tok Tsèpa's words:

Ordinary mind awakens in the center of the heart.
When the six modes of consciousness are purified, great
  bliss is unceasing.

Some refer to that ordinary mind as "natural luminosity," some as
"ground mahamudra," and so forth; there are countless names. In
tantric scriptures, it is well known as the "co-emergent" or "innate"
nature. This is explained as the co-emergence of emptiness, the
object, and natural luminosity, the subject. However, in experiential language, it is said to be a suddenly arisen awareness of mere
unimpeded understanding, a vivid knowing. To not recognize this
is samsara; to know it is nirvana. It does not fall into any extreme;
its essence is great bliss. This perceiver is indivisibly unified with
the emptiness that is supreme in all ways. Apart from just that, it
cannot be expressed in words. From *Expressing the Names of Manjushri* (*Manjushri Nama Sangiti*):

> It is inexpressible in words. It is the supreme cause of all
> expression.

Therefore, this is the ground of both samsara and nirvana. From
the *Condensed Hevajra Tantra*:

> This itself is called samsara; this itself is nirvana.

And:

> One is a samsaric being due to confusion about this.
> Without confusion, samsara is purified. Therefore, this
> ground is explained to be the single basis of samsara and
> nirvana.

You may think that explaining the natural mind as a suddenly
arisen awareness lacks reasoning. However, this "suddenly arisen
awareness" is not a newly arisen thing. From when the prior thought
has ceased until the next thought has arisen, there is no obscuration that appears. Therefore, it is expressed in that way. Although
suchness continually appears at all times, it is usually not manifest
due to being obscured by the web of conceptuality.

For a worldly analogy, it is like the sun continually shining from
morning until night during a storm. When the clouds part a little,
the sun is said to newly shine and when obscured, it is said to not
shine. In this regard, Jetsun Milarepa said:

> In the gap between the former thought and following
> thought, original wakefulness continuously appears.
> Taste it for yourself!

Is not this luminosity the same as the brightness that lights up
the day here? No. The nature of daytime is merely called "luminosity." Furthermore, this awareness is also called "instantaneous
pure awareness." As for its meaning: While not extending from

one moment to the next, it is in the following moment exactly as it was in the previous moment. It is not possible for it to change into something else! Thus, it is given that label of instantaneous awareness. This agrees extremely well with what Jetsun Maitreya said (in the *Mahayana Uttaratantra Shastra*):

> Just as it was before, so it is after. It has the nature of being unchanging . . .

"Instantaneous awareness" cannot be said to have the characteristic of impermanence.

When presented in accordance with the sutric path, these aspects are explained from the point of view of negation. When in accord with the tantric path, those same aspects are taught from the point of view of affirmation. Both of these are merely reified explanations. Even the perfect buddhas are at a loss for words in expressing how the meaning actually is! From *Accomplishing Suchness*:

> That very king, the great bliss of all beings,
> Is free from causality, yet always arising.
> Whenever it is to be articulated,
> The Omniscient One is always at a loss for words.
> May it be victorious!

From the *Treasury of Dohas*:

> The genuine nature cannot be indicated by anyone.

Therefore, to understand this crucial point in this manner, it is pointless to debate good and bad in relation to the view. Until realizing the true nature, everything is only a mental fabrication, so you cannot rely on it! When one has realized the true nature, apart from mere words, it is impossible to be out of harmony with the meaning. For those who wish to resolve the view as it actually is, direct realization is necessary. Thus, it is said that "the view and realization are interrelated." As it is said:

> The difference in this approach is that the view dawns
> from within realization,
> Without relying on scripture and reasoning.

This is an incredibly crucial point! Therefore, in this yoga of simplicity, by determining the unreality of the knowing quality—the subject—the true existence of the object is automatically destroyed. Then everything manifests like an illusion. This is therefore an authentic insight—free of the concepts of apprehended and apprehender. This is the explanation of the yoga of simplicity. As the Victorious One himself proclaimed:

> Profound, peaceful, free of elaborations,
> Luminous, and unconditioned—I have found a nectar-like
> Dharma.
> Whoever I teach it to will not be able to understand,
> So I will remain silent here in the forest.

3. One Taste

> When the innate nature of mind is known in the midst of
> appearances,
> And the way appearances arise is realized within mind,
> The division between appearances and mind falls away.
> This is the recognition of one taste.

The realization of all appearances being the mind itself, at the very moment of just appearing, is called "knowing the innate nature of mind in the midst of appearances." The radiance of the mind essence appearing as all aspects is called "realizing the way appearances arise within the mind." The former is the one taste of multiplicity, and the latter is one taste arising as multiplicity. From the *Treasury of Dohas*:

> All the three realms without exception acquire the color of great attachment. . . .

And:

> However much the mind projects, all is the nature of the protector.
> Water and waves—are they different?

One might consider that when meditating on simplicity, one either realizes or does not realize that all appearances are the mind itself. If one does realize this, then it is not different from the meditation of one taste. Since the special feature of one taste is the recognition of all appearances as mind, what then is the need for having both these yogas? If one does not realize this, one also does not realize that all phenomena lack inherent self-existence, and thus how does this qualify as authentic simplicity?

There is truth to this. However, at the time of simplicity, all thoughts that grasp at phenomena, from form until omniscience, are determined as lacking inherent existence. Therefore, this is posited as "the determination that all phenomena lack inherent reality." However, perceptual objects do not appear as meditation. When the subject is vanquished, grasping to the true existence of objects is naturally destroyed. Then objects arise like an illusion.

At that time, through having all appearances pointed out as being mind, "outer" perceptual objects without exception are known as mental forms. Thus, all apparent objects without exception are realized as being "inside" one's own mind. At this time, the experience is called "perceptual objects and mind becoming one taste," or "appearances dawning as meditation."

When this happens, one is able to do anything with appearances, such as passing through walls and mountains without obstruction and so forth. This is thus known as "appearances and mind being mingled." Otherwise, saying "mind and appearances are mingled," while understanding in a way akin to salt and water being mixed together, is incorrect. Accordingly, Shawari Wangchuk proclaimed:

> If one realizes the nature of mind, this is mahamudra.
> Whatever appears is not different from one's own mind.

Furthermore:

> If you realize the nature, everything is like that.
> No one can find something separate from that.

Furthermore:

> At the very moment of merely appearing,
> Nothing whatsoever is established.
> This lack of any true existence
> Arises as mere appearance.
> Thus, this is the unity of empty appearances,
> Or the co-emergence of appearances and emptiness.
>
> The unity of the object—great bliss,
> With the subject—emptiness endowed with all supreme
>   aspects,
> Is the unity of bliss and emptiness,
> Or their co-emergence.
>
> The relative truth is the radiance or expressive power
> Arising as the illusory body.
> The ultimate truth is unwavering
> From the luminous nature or ground.

That these two can never be differentiated as separate
Is the meaning of unity.
This is the unity or indivisibility of the two truths.

In the state of emptiness without characteristics,
To train in virtues such as generosity and so forth,
Is well known as the unity of method and wisdom.

Furthermore, precious Kagyu masters of the past have quoted the *Sutra That Teaches All Phenomena Are Unarisen*, which states, "All phenomena are the essence of attachment." Attachment is proclaimed to be nirvana, likewise anger and delusion. "Enlightenment is the very abiding of these," and, "Enlightenment and attachment are not dual." In line with these and other such quotations, with the realization that all thoughts that grasp at phenomena, from form to omniscience, have a completely pure nature and do not veer even the slightest bit from this completely pure nature, there are teachings such as thoughts are dharmakaya and afflictions are wisdom.

It is impossible that this completely pure nature changes within the contexts of ground, path, and fruition. Thus, at the time of the ground, thoughts are dharmakaya and at the time of the path, there is no purpose in explaining otherwise; therefore, there is no difference in the way it is during the times of ground and path. It is indeed the case that the dharmakaya dawning or not depends on the mind of the individual. However, the dharmakaya not appearing occurs due to not recognizing what is as it is. This "not recognizing" can never be found to exist, and so this very not-knowing is also unwavering from the dharmakaya. Saraha says:

It is like when he is at home but she goes looking for him
    outside;
Or when she has seen her husband but asks the neighbors
    where he is.

It is like having seen the spouse that you are looking for, but not recognizing her, and then going around to other people, asking, "Where is she?" Although you have not recognized her, she has not become anyone else! From the *Hevajra Tantra*:

> Realization does not happen by abandoning samsara
> And finding nirvana somewhere else.

From the *Heart Sutra* (*Hirdaya Sutra*):

> Form is emptiness. Emptiness is form.
> Emptiness is not other than form.
> Form is also not other than emptiness.

From the *King of Samadhi Sutra*:

> "Form is one thing; the essence of form is a different thing"—do not see in this way. "The essence of form is one thing; the Tathagata is a different thing"—do not see in this way. That which is the essence of form and that which is the Tathagata have a nondual nature. If a bodhisattva, a great being, sees in this way, they are engaging in authentic awareness of individual phenomena.

The Victorious One has thus extensively explained this point.

To those who view the teaching that thoughts are dharmakaya as faulty, we ask this question: Is there a common ground of appearances for ordinary and noble beings? If not, in line with Maitreya's remark, "This is experienced as an unappetizing taste or as supremely delicious. . . ." and the unappetizing taste would have to be the singular experience of the buddhas.

If there is a common ground, to ordinary beings it is solely impure appearances, to yogins it is yogic experience, and to buddhas it is the dharmakaya. We and everyone else accept these as common appearances. However, in these contexts, if the ground of appearances is not the dharmakaya, and yet the buddhas see it as the dharmakaya, the consequence would be that the buddhas would have distorted vision. Would that not be an utter absurdity? If we give the enlightened beings' experience more credence, we have to say that the common basis is the dharmakaya.

Furthermore, in some of the omniscient Dolpopa's pith instruction texts, there is criticism of the assertion that thoughts are the dharmakaya. However, he holds that:

> Aspects of samsara appear and yet are not samsara.
> Varieties of thoughts appear and yet are not thoughts.

This they (the Jonang) verbally accept as their own excellent tradition.

All the various manifestations of thoughts are called "thoughts." Apart from that, toward the completely pure nature of thoughts, there is no one at all who calls that a thought. Also, those who assert thoughts as the dharmakaya do so through considering that although the varieties of thoughts appear, the essence is the dharmakaya. This is how they present thoughts as the dharmakaya. Therefore, I do not see Dolpopa's position as a refutation.

Some among the Sakya tradition hold that the form aggregate is Vairochana, the earth element is Buddha Locana, delusion is the original wisdom of basic space, and so forth. They also accept the view of the indivisibility of samsara and nirvana, but then disparage such principles as thoughts being the dharmakaya and others. If an intelligent person encounters this, they will see that these views comprise a complete set of prerequisites to directly cause their own contradiction!

My own position is that the point of mental certainty of those who accept thoughts as the dharmakaya and the explanations of the definitive meaning from among those who do not accept thoughts as dharmakaya are the same ultimate reference points for those learned masters. As long as there is grasping to "thoughts" and "dharmakaya," one does not go beyond concepts. When the conceptual mind that clings to good and bad is destroyed, one is liberated from wondering if it's dharmakaya or not. Therefore, it is evident that it's valid to follow whichever position is more convenient for oneself. This yoga of the unity of the path of training authentically realizes the equal taste of all phenomena, and so it is called "the yoga of one-taste." From the *Hevajra Tantra*:

> Equal taste is said to be equivalent to
> The "equality" that comes from meditating on suchness.
> The continuous state of that equality is called its "taste."

> This equality of one taste meditation
> Will be expressed according to its ultimate meaning:

> All beings arise from me.
> The three sacred places also arise from me.
> All this is pervaded by me.
> Do not see the nature of beings as different.

4. Nonmeditation

When one does not waver from the flow of suchness in
   post-meditation,
And compassion spontaneously overflows in meditative
   composure,
The division between meditation and post-meditation falls away.
This is the recognition of nonmeditation.

In all situations, to be unwavering from the seamless experience of suchness, is called "unwavering from the flow of suchness in post-meditation." The activity of accomplishing the happiness and benefit of sentient beings as long as samsara remains, through the nature of great compassion of that very suchness, is called "the overflowing of compassion in meditative composure."

Engaging in benefitting others through great compassion is merely given the label of "post-meditation," but actually it is only ever a meditative state. This approach is called the "unity of the two kayas." Without wavering from the dharmakaya that benefits oneself, the form kayas are emanated that benefit others. Because this emanation of the form kayas that benefit others does not waver from the dharmakaya that benefits oneself, it is explained to be a unity. Furthermore, in the *Sublime Continuum* (*Mahayana Uttaratantra Shastra*):

> Without wavering from the dharmakaya,
> A variety of emanations,
> Actually take birth . . . and so on.

From the *Treasury of Dohas*:

> The sublime stalk of the nondual mind,
> Pervades the three realms without exception.
> It holds the flowers of compassion and
> The fruits of altruism.

In this vein, it is similar to "the path of no more learning" in the Paramita vehicle, which comes about through the power of ending the path and finishing the practice. Here, by the power of extinguishing the meditator and the meditation object, there is the so-called yoga of nonmeditation. The *Hevajra Tantra* discusses this topic as well:

> There is no meditation,
> And no meditator either.
> There is no deity and also no mantra.
>
> Within this nature of no elaboration
> Is the authentic abode of deity and mantra;

Of the great beings Vairochana, Akshobya,
Amoghasiddhi, Ratnasambhava, and Amitabha.

Also, from the *Glorious Compendium* (*Shri Samaja*) and the
Kalachakra Tantra:

When there is nothing substantial,
There is no meditation.
The real activity of meditation
Is no meditation at all.
Thus, because entities are insubstantial,
Meditation has no reference point.

These quotations clearly explain how it is at the time of fruition. In
Venerable Saraha's *Play Doha* (*Sikhara Doha*):

What is the taste of the innate's nectar?
That unceasing nature is like
The flow of a river and the sky.

It abides at all times, unmoving.
The logical mind, the follower of thoughts,
Can never know it.

Inconceivable, it is never an object.
Without an object, how can there be meditation?
It is also not something called nonmeditation.

Whoever has written about this metaphor of the meaning
Has a mind equal to the mind of the Buddha!

The stages of the four yogas have thus been explained for those of
weak intellect in an easily understandable way.

This was composed by the monk Pema Karpo in the shrine room called The Sacred Place of the Teachings, on the very top of the great temple of Tashi Thongmun.

May this bring vast benefit to the teachings! *Maṅgalam!*

The Blessed Vase

The Meaning of the Mahamudra of
Four Syllables Condensed to Its Essence

Tsele Natsok Rangdrol

Gurus of the practice lineage,
who have given up all faults and acquired all qualities,
I offer you respect
from the very depths of my heart.

Here I will attempt to give a mnemonic list of the practical instruc-
tions of this lineage.

As commanded by you, Ku Rinpoche, I will present the essential
points of Mahamudra with which to stabilize one's practice.

Generally speaking, whichever spiritual approach you choose, the
destination is the same. However, as you have prior acquaintance
with the Mahamudra of Four Syllables, if I base my explanation
upon that tradition it will serve as a swift conduit to receive tre-
mendous blessings. Even though you have obviously studied these
teachings extensively and realized them well, I will here present
you with the key points of essential practice to serve as an aid to
memory.

What we refer to as four syllables can just as easily be listed as
four points that include (1) cutting the root of the mind, (2) pre-
senting the methods of resting meditation as a path, (3) removing
deviations from that path, and (4) the way to carry the practice
into one's activities.

Tsele Natsok Rangdrol (b. 1608)

Tsele Natsok Rangdrol was recognized as a body emanation of
the great translator Vairotsana, and also as a reincarnation of the
Drukpa master Götsangpa, an emanation of Milarepa. He was an
extraordinary scholar who mastered Sutra and Tantra, and then
perfected his realization of Dzogchen and Mahamudra in retreat.

1. Cutting the Root of the Mind

The practice consists of seeking the mind's origin, abode, and destination; to look for its characteristics—its color, shape, existence or lack thereof, its permanence or voidness—until you reach a conclusion. It can be done in a common way by utilizing much thought, analysis, and reason, or in a unique way by applying the key points of posture and gaze, allowing your mind to simply rest in its own space, to literally drop. When your mind is left in this way, use your awareness to meticulously investigate just what is abiding, where, and how.

When you give rise to a movement of mind, say a sudden proliferation of thought, at that very instant look where it came from, how it moved, and what actually moved. Similarly, if your mind suddenly goes to a place such as your homeland, does your mind actually go there, or does the country come to you? In this and similar ways, investigate. Investigate with great endeavor and see if the investigator and that which is being investigated are one and the same or different.

Some may say that to simply know that these are not established, to simply say "I cannot establish anything" or "I cannot find anything" is to cut the root of the mind. However, in the practice lineage, until you have gone beyond mere terms, such as "established or not," or "found or not," you will not have directly realized the naked awareness—the essential luminosity, the natural state beyond the mind, and the essential emergence of appearance, awareness, and emptiness—that is to be recognized here. As the glorious Khachopa writes:

> Initially, the original mind is primordially pure,
> In-between, its abode is realized to be empty,
> And lastly, there has never been a place for it to go.

> Its essence is beyond all characteristics, color, and shape,
> And it has nothing upon which to grasp.

This insight, cutting the mind at its very root,
Is simply the recognition of the mind's nature.

Do not be satisfied with mere theory. Apply yourself with diligence and single pointedly supplicate your root and lineage gurus: "May a faultless practice arise within me!"

2. Presenting the Methods of Resting Meditation as a Path

Resting meditation can also be referred to as calm abiding, however, this is not the common practice going by that name. Rather it is the sustaining of the rootless co-emergent union mentioned earlier in which insight and stillness are accomplished together. As Khachopa says:

Remain like the sun in a cloudless sky.

Bring forth an experience that is brilliant and clear, beyond the obscurations of obliviousness, distraction, and dullness.

Be like a magnificent garuda soaring in the sky.

Go beyond the obscurations of coarse behavior, distraction, and doubt.

Be naturally settled, serene, and unperturbed as the ocean's great depths.

When agitated by discursive thoughts both gross and subtle, do not allow yourself to be moved from natural and clear awareness, the natural state of the ground. But rather you should:

Remain like a child looking around a temple.

When objects of the six senses arise, do not block them, remain clear. Do not give rise to the idea of good and bad, along with the proliferation of wishing to enhance the former and reject the latter, remain experiencing all as of a single taste.

Be like the traces left by a bird in flight.

Whatever thought arises will naturally fade away, as will its prior thought, afterthought, and so on, like a drawing made in water. There is no need for pointless effort to be made here, be carefree and let go.

Be like the gentle unfolding of a cotton flower.

Allow the artificial constrictions and knots of your body and mind to free themselves—to loosen, relax, and become serene. Within this state your mind will become clear and brilliant. To use analysis at this point is a total waste of time.

For beginners, it is essential to initially begin with a lot of short meditation sessions, and during the breaks to look well and see if they can find any difference in the mind during meditation and post-meditation sessions. Naturally they will come to the point where they will see no distinction.

3. Removing Deviations from the Path

Khachopa states:

> It is a mistake to hope for Buddhahood, just as it is a mistake to fear samsara.

Here there are two points. Firstly, the hope to achieve a pleasant state of Buddhahood reflects a failure to recognize the spontaneous presence of the indivisible three kayas, the immediate mind, and thus one seeks Buddhahood elsewhere. Similarly, to imagine samsara as a place of terrible migration existing in some direction, an awful place full of suffering one is fearful of being born into, reveals a failure to understand that both samsara and nirvana are the play of the mind. To adhere to such a dichotomy, a difference between mind and its object, is to abide in an object/subject fixation and to deviate from the view. Similarly:

> To grasp at external appearances is to stray.

Ordinary people fixate upon and grasp at things, non-Buddhist practitioners grasp at the acts of a creator, hearers and solitary realizers grasp at atoms, and practitioners of Mantra who do not understand the union of the two truths view the deities and mandalas as real, and then grasp at and become addicted to their visionary appearances.

Addiction to internal meditative experiences is to stray. Signs of progress in your practice can be measured by means of the signs of the path—bliss, clarity, and no thoughts—and also by the ten signs, the development of clairvoyance, magical powers, and so on. When these occur, do not focus upon them and they will pass. If you are delighted to see such signs, become conceited, and are addicted to them, your practice will be ruined. Because of this, these experiences are potentially very dangerous.

> To be content with mere theory is to stray.

To think: "I have received these profound instructions. I have studied them, I know them, and I know how to practice them. How wonderful!" is to invite pride and conceit. By not practicing, the instructions will become an obstacle to you.

> To ignore the collection of merit is to stray.

Even though verbally clever and confident in your understanding of the ultimate, you must refrain from speaking ill of the compounded virtues of cause and effect, dependent arising, and practices that use characteristics. Some say these can be done away with, but this is just evil, empty prattle. To avoid the pitfalls of these deviations to your view, meditation, and conduct, train—as many have done—in both method and wisdom, which are to be unified.

4. The Way to Carry the Practice into One's Activities

Here there are six points.

> 1. Seal daytime appearances.

There is nothing to speak of outside of your meditation experience. During both meditation and post-meditation sessions you must continually recall how all appearances, sounds, and thoughts are simply manifestations of the natural clarity of your own awareness, until you come to realize it yourself.

> 2. Between dawn and dusk allow objects of desire to become your friends.

Whatever you like—food, drink, clothes, relaxing at home, and so forth—be sure not to enjoy them as an ordinary person would. Remain free from the bondage of addiction toward all that is offered to your senses. See them all as ultimately the play of suchness, and conventionally enjoy them as offerings for the gurus and yidam deities.

> 3. At dusk gather your senses into the ground.

As you retire for the night do not give rise to a continual chain of delusion and thought. Rather, fall asleep within the all-pervasive natural state, the primordial ground.

> 4. At midnight, place all within a vase.

There are various pith instructions for placing the mind within a vase, according to both the new and old schools of translation. Here we will place the mind states of appearance, increase, and attainment within the unelaborated vase of suchness, subject to neither restriction nor extremes. To enter and settle within the expanse of the great empty luminosity free from all entry, its branch method is to visualize your guru clearly within a luminous sphere at your heart and train in falling asleep without allowing your mind to wander.

5. At dawn maintain wisdom's clarity.

When you awaken do not give rise to a stream of discursive thoughts. Maintain the essence of your session and remain within the continuum of wisdom.

6. Send the suchness of death into utter lucidity.

At the time of death do not give in to all kinds of thoughts—what you have done, what you could have done, and similar heavy, restless notions and so on—instead recognize the self-appearing signs of birth and death. Do not envision something moving to another place, rather within your own awareness, the empty and clear state of suchness, remain utterly open, unobstructed, and without defilement. In this way the luminosities of the ground and path will meet like the water of a river emptying into the ocean, or like the space inside a vase merging with outside space when the vase breaks.

The essential practice points of the Mahamudra of Four Syllables are hereby summarized. However, it is essential to lead a beginner progressively. Begin by explaining the preliminary contemplations: The rarity of the freedoms and endowments that comprise a precious human life, impermanence, action, cause and effect, and so on. Thereafter, teach the meditations of refuge, bodhichitta, the hundred-syllable mantra of Vajrasattva, mandala offering, and guru yoga. These stages of practice are found in all Mahamudra instruction manuals.

It is inappropriate for a guru to thoroughly teach a student who may have requested teachings but who does not get their meaning, or who requests them simply for the sake of it. Rather, meditation instructions should be given in accordance with the individual needs of each practitioner.

For the practice of Mahamudra to be fruitful, it is imperative to exert yourself not only in the actual meditation but also in the following ways. Begin a session of meditation by giving rise to the thought of bodhichitta: "The purpose of my entering into this profound practice is to be able to place each and every being existing throughout the very reaches of space in the state of the indivisible four kayas." Similarly, at the conclusion of a practice session recite prayers of dedication, such that you may be able to swiftly achieve these aims.

Concerning the generation-stage meditation, when taking food and drink as a path reflect that your aggregates, elements, and sense bases are primordially the spontaneously present deities and mantras. At nighttime, when gathering all within a vase, remember to practice guru yoga, and visualize your master within your heart. As is said:

> Bodhichitta, the yidam deity,
> Guru, Mahamudra,
> And dedication are the teachings to practice.

This here is the profound path of the Fivefold Mahamudra. Thus, it is not wrong to say that if the lion's roar of Mahamudra is devoid of the five-fold practices, it is as if muted. By putting this compendium of essential points into continual practice, such that the wisdom wheel keeps on turning, may you come to slice through the net of existence. Through the stainless pith instructions coming from those such as Tilopa and Naropa, down to the king of Dharma, Tsuglag Gyatso, the blessings of this, the lineage of union, are gathered here in this fine vase. I offer it to you, the supreme emanation, Mipham Gonpo, with the hope that it may enhance and assist your innermost heart practice. By this merit may each and every being throughout space perfect the practice of Mahamudra and awaken to enlightenment.

The renunciant Natsok Rangdrol wrote this in the wilds of the Vulture Cave Hermitage without any difficulty.

ESSENCE OF REFINED GOLD

Practical Advice for the View, Meditation,
and Conduct of Mahamudra

THE THIRD KHAMTRUL KUNGA TENZIN

Namo guru prabhā karāya!

Lordly Drukpa, embodiment of all unmistaken refuges,
Even though we are never separate, I continually supplicate you.

For those of you inclined to practice the Dharma, I offer these words
from the bottom of my heart:

Generally speaking, it is very hard to attain a human body and, more to the point, to acquire one possessing the three vows is next to impossible. However, when we have one if we do not use it to practice the Dharma, gaining another in the future will be extremely unlikely—put it to use with prostrations and circumambulations.

Your sworn enemy, Yama, the Lord of Death, approaches, his time of arrival unknown. Even though you intend to practice the Dharma, death may lay waste to your plans, therefore practice virtue and abandon negative actions right now!

If even hearing of the plight of those born in the three lower realms causes your heart to quiver, imagine what it would be like to actually be born there.... What would you do? Considering this, avoid negative deeds as you would poison.

Pray to the Three Jewels—which are never actually apart from you—from the very depths of your heart. It is only they who are able to protect you from the seemingly endless pain of samsara.

The Third Khamtrul Kunga Tenzin (1680–1728)

The Third Khamtrul Kunga Tenzin realized the nature of mind when he was four years old. In retreat, he had a vision of Guru Padmasambhava in which he received prophecies of the sorrows that would befall the Tibetan people, and the command to leave retreat and benefit many beings through performing religious dance festivals and particular sadhanas.

Finding all beings within samsara's six realms to be miserable, and recognizing that each and every one has, at one time or another, been your parents, dedicate the results of your Dharma practice to them.

Visualize your perfect guru seated upon your crown and supplicate him from the very depths of your heart. Imagine he melts into light and dissolves into you, his wisdom mind merging with yours. Remain with this experience and watch your mind, without changing anything.

Rest and observe its outer, inner, and secret movement without altering anything. Mind does not exist as it has no substance, similarly it does not not exist as it can think about all sorts of things; sometimes it stays and sometimes it goes—watch it without break.

> The empty essence of your mind is Amitabha—the
> dharmakaya,
> Its luminous nature is Avalokiteshvara—the sambhogakaya,
> And its myriad projections of thought are
> Padmasambhava—the nirmanakaya.

If you recognize the five poisonous emotions when they arise, they are the five Buddha families. When the mind is particularly lucid, look at the nature of that luminosity—this is the mahamudra of luminous emptiness. When the mind is particularly blissful, look at the nature of that bliss—this is the Great Perfection of bliss-emptiness. When the mind is particularly empty, stare into the face of that emptiness—this is the empty awareness of the Great Middle Way. When the mind is particularly fearful, look at the nature of the fear—this is what is to be dissolved in the profound practice of cutting demons, chöd. When you don't see the mind as anything whatsoever, this is the emptiness of mind, the prajnaparamita.

Whether moving or at rest, look at the mind—all activity will be the ultimate circumambulation. Whether eating or drinking, look at the mind—this is the inexhaustible feast of the ganachakra. Whether resting or sleeping, look at the mind—this is the pith instruction to experience sleep as natural luminosity. The profundity of the recitation practices of approach and accomplishment comes from watching the mind; it will also reverse the obstacles of Mara, should that be necessary.

Right now, no matter what fleeting thoughts may run through your mind, resolve that your meditation will last the length of your life. Whether socializing and chatting among friends, watching entertainment, or when busy with the affairs of your life, never fall under the sway of distraction—never be distracted from the nature of the mind. This is what it means to have a profound meditation.

Do not forget this instruction; keep each and every point in mind and your practice will become stable and strong. Use it to repeatedly bring your mind under control and you will become very accustomed to the uninterrupted flow of meditation, like the course of a wide river.

This advice, an oral instruction like refined gold, was written by the reincarnation of Karma Tenpel, Ngawang Kunga Tenzin Gelek from Kham, and meant for all: lay or clergy—male or female.

The Two Truths in Union

A Practice for Fulfilling Wishes and Admitting
Faults to All Those Worthy of Veneration

The Third Khamtrul Kunga Tenzin

Namo buddha dharma saṅgha guru deva ḍākinī dharmapālebhyaḥ!

All phenomena of samsara and nirvana
Are but appearances arising interdependently.
They are thus unborn, primordially pure, and occur in the expanse
of unity.[26]
I bow to the indestructible mind.

Those beings whose good fortune and virtues
Have brought them into the supreme Vajrayana,
Should exert themselves in this fulfillment and confession
In order to clear obscurations and actualize the four kayas.

The practice has three parts: (1) the preparation, (2) the actual practice, and (3) the conclusion.

Preparation

In a pleasant and clean place, display representations of the Three Jewels and the Three Roots. Arrange, beautifully and properly, whatever offerings you have for the outer, inner, and secret practices, as well as any ritual objects that will be needed. Either do the preliminaries as indicated in the corresponding texts or, instead, generate a vast mind of completely pure bodhichitta.

ACTUAL PRACTICE

The actual practice has seven parts.

1. Blessing the Offerings

Sprinkle the offerings with purifying water.

OM ĀḤ HŪṂ
The essence of one's mind is the dharmakaya,
Its lucid nature is the sambhogakaya,
And the manifold compassionate energy is the dance of the
    nirmanakaya.

The seed syllables of the three kayas
Perfectly cleanse and purify the offerings,
Turning them into the most exquisite sensual objects, made of
    light yet potent.
Spontaneously formed, they fill the sky
As infinite clouds of Samantabhadra's offerings.

2. Generating the Assembly of Samaya Deities

HRĪḤ
In the unchangeable dharmadhatu, free from mind-made
    limitations,27
There is no observable object whatsoever,
Yet its free-flowing radiance shines everywhere in distinct forms.
To be with the two truths in union is the supreme path.
Thus, from the expanse of the unfabricated essence of mind,
And its natural lucidity in continuous undistracted awareness,
The elements of the visualization take form.

In this vast space where development and completion are
    indivisible,[28]
All the countless worlds are pure buddha fields,
With dense banks of luminous lights of the five rainbow colors,
Among which are the precious Three Jewels of the past,
Those who are now in the ten directions,
And those who will come in the future.
There are also all the root and lineage gurus, whose forms are a
    blessing,
The deities of the ocean of mandalas, who are the sources of
    siddhis,
And dakinis and Dharma protectors, the embodiments of
    buddha activity.

All the worthy refuges are there,
And also each and every form of sentient being,
My kind mothers as infinite as the sky in number.
Primordially pure, we are by nature like the deities:
Perfect lucidity in natural flow.

3. Inviting the Assembly of Wisdom Deities

HRĪḤ
In the great unborn and perfect mandala,
Union, separation, and all other extreme views are unknown.
In that all-pervading space
Even the terms "samaya deities" and "wisdom deities" do not
    exist.

Nevertheless, O embodiments of the three kayas, O assembled
    refuges,
When we invite you with faith and yearning,
Through your nonreferential compassion, please come
To us who have dualistic perception.

4. Requesting Them to Remain and Paying Homage

Please remain in the state of nonduality,
Here, in this self-existing mandala of emanated deities.
We prostrate continuously to you
With impartial devotion embracing all.

5. Making Offerings and Fulfilling Wishes

HRĪḤ
In the true nature of ultimate reality
There is neither offering, nor offeror, nor any such distinctions.
On experiencing the relative plane of conditioned phenomena,
The myriad things are possible.

All that exists arises from emptiness,
But although it arises, its essence is completely empty.
Phenomena and emptiness are inseparable like the moon in
    water,
Or an image in a spotless mirror;
If one examines them, they are unreal appearances;
Without doing so, one is seduced by them.

To you refuges, the play of the dharmakaya,
There is neither a recipient to be pleased, nor an offering that
    pleases.
Nevertheless, for the realization of the inherent two kayas,
The result of practicing the two accumulations together,
We shall fulfill your wishes and make offerings.

All the galaxies of the universe;
Drinking water, bathing water, flowers, incense,
Light, perfume, food, and music;
The seven treasures of a universal monarch,[29] the eight auspicious
    symbols,[30]

The eight auspicious objects,[31] the five sense pleasures,
The most fabulous riches possible;[32]
All the beings inhabiting these galaxies,
Our bodies, possessions, and merit of the three times;
Mentally taking possession of everything in existence,
We offer it all with unshakable faith.

Amrita made with the eight main and one thousand secondary
    ingredients,
Red lakes of many kinds of *rakta*,
And gigantic, magnificent *tormas*.
We make all these offerings,
Inexhaustible and infinite in number.

The five sense organs, melted fat, liquid amrita,
Great flesh, thighbone trumpets, secret drums,
The implements for practicing, for calling you, representing you,
And the things that fulfill your wishes,
We completely offer them to you!

Inconceivable numbers of exceptional offering goddesses,
Who are perfect in all the marks that distinguish them,
We also offer to you
As bases for the great bliss of union.

In short, these outer, inner, and secret offerings,
Each multiplied into myriad wish-fulfilling objects,
Fill the whole universe.

Through mudra, mantra, and samadhi, we evolve toward
    perfection,
And above all we avoid wrongdoing.
Having entered the gate of the three vows,
We shall diligently follow the disciplines.

With these good actions that bring our body, speech, and mind
Into the spheres of the deity's body, mantra, and wisdom,
We fulfill the wishes of the Three Jewels
And the wishes of the root and lineage gurus.
We fulfill the wishes of the yidams
And those of the dakinis and dharmapalas.
And we also fulfill the wishes of the six kinds of beings.

We thus worship, make offerings, and praise;
Please accept these, considering me and all beings with love.
May your sacred wishes be fulfilled.
May the power of these actions
Purify all negativities, obscurations, and transgressions of
    beginningless samsara.
Please bless us so that we may complete
The supreme accumulations of merit and wisdom.

6. The Ultimate Offering and Fulfillment of Wishes

ĀḤ
To the all-pervading lord, one's own mind,
We offer the drink of immaculate bodhichitta water,
The bathing water of primordial purity, the flowers of self-arising,
The incense of natural flow, the lamp of luminosity,
The perfume of letting be, the food of mindfulness,
And the sounds of nonmeditation;
The galaxies of thoughts, sights, and sounds,
Recognized as emptiness;
Oceans of the fabulous riches in samsara and nirvana;
Of self-liberated situations;
And the implements for practicing, representing, fulfilling, and
    so forth,
Of the ever-present unwavering samadhi.

We also offer the amrita of experience,
The rakta of passions used as the path,
The torma of perfect realization of things as they are,
And the secret consort of untainted great bliss.

We make all these offerings without conceptualizing the three
    spheres,
In the state of co-emergent wisdom of nonduality,
Where all phenomena in the material and sentient realms
Are always the mahamudra, beyond change and transition.

The wishes of the deities of unborn awareness are fulfilled
By knowing the nature.
The wishes of the deities of unimpeded phenomena are fulfilled
By the self-liberation of dualistic fixation.
The wishes of the deities of the all-pervading dharmadhatu are
    fulfilled
By non-action beyond concepts.
And the wishes of the deities within the equality of samsara and
    nirvana are fulfilled
When purity is all-encompassing.

7. Admitting Faults

HRĪḤ
In the play of the single sphere,[33]
The transparency where inner and outer are indistinguishable,
Dualistic distinctions are rootless and without foundation.
Nevertheless, in the temporary conceptual sphere of labels,
You, supreme lords, emerge.
When we admit our faults to you,
Please regard us with the all-seeing eyes of your loving-kindness
And give thought to us with great compassion.

All beings have the buddha essence
And are by nature purity itself.
Still, within beginningless samsara,
Clouded by karma and afflictive emotions,
And dominated by ignorance and delusion,
We have only created daydreams and wrongdoings.
Every single action that results in suffering,
This we openly admit.

Only through the strength of our merit,
Do we now have all the conditions for Dharma practice.
But since our propensities and bad habits are full blown,
We continue doing the wrong things.

We have squandered the opportunities of this human birth,
Acquired this time only;
This we openly admit.
All existence rapidly changes and dies,
Yet we have held it as permanent;
This we openly admit.

We have misconstrued
The unequivocal karmic law of cause and effect;
This we openly admit.
We have not understood
That the nature of samsara is suffering;
This we openly admit.

This life, which is like a dream,
We have regarded as real;
This we openly admit.
We have become attached
To sense pleasures, deceptive things as they are;
This we openly admit.
We have yearned for places and friends,

While connections with them are so fleeting;
This we openly admit.

At last, able to choose between happiness and misery,
We were careless in our choice;
This we openly admit.
Our trust in the Three Jewels, the constant refuge,
Has faltered;
This we openly admit.

Our commitments to individual liberation
Have been weakened;
This we openly admit.
We have not put into practice
All the disciplines of the bodhisattva;
This we openly admit.
We have neglected
The sets of tantric samayas;
This we openly admit.

We have regarded the root and lineage gurus, who are buddhas,
As ordinary beings;
This we openly admit.
We have not persevered
In the supplications of the profound path of devotion;
This we openly admit.
We have neither taken to heart the pith teachings
Of true meaning nor those of the secret path;[34]
This we openly admit.

In development, completion, and mantra recitation of the yidam,
We have been lax;
This we openly admit.
The invocation for the activity of the ocean of protectors
Has been irregular;

This we openly admit.
We have not practiced the pure perception
In which sights and sounds are the display of purity;
This we openly admit.

We have not seen our original face,
The primordially pure natural condition;
This we openly admit.
We have tainted with alterations
The pristine cognizance free of concept;
This we openly admit.
Mindfulness, the heart of the path,
Has lapsed into delusion;
This we openly admit.

Although all thoughts are the display of the basic nature,
We have blocked some and pursued others;
This we openly admit.
The objects of the five senses, which are the natural expression of
    emptiness,
We have grasped as solid;
This we openly admit.
In all types of internal and external experiences,
We have been governed by desire and aggression;
This we openly admit.

We have deemed significant
The highs and lows of meditative experiences;
This we openly admit.
The ordinary mind, which is primordial awareness,
We have covered over with "good" thoughts;
This we openly admit.
We have meditated conceptually on that which is beyond
The watcher-and-watched of the conceptual mind;
This we openly admit.

During post-meditation of self-occurring self-liberation,
We have lapsed into ensuing knowledge;[35]
This we openly admit.
In the carefree expression of emptiness there are no preferences,
Yet we have been partial;[36]
This we openly admit.
We have contaminated the nongrasping and carefree natural flow
With our habitual patterns;
This we openly admit.

We are not yet convinced
That the Three Roots are entirely within the essence of our mind;
This we openly admit.
Emptiness and compassion, which are indivisible,
Have been experienced as separate;
This we openly admit.
We do not know how to create the conditions
To accomplish the form kayas for the benefit of others;[37]
This we openly admit.

We have not actualized the fruition of the path,
The equality of samsara and nirvana;
This we openly admit.
We have not arrived at the expanse where the whole phenomenal
    world
Is the mandala of the three kayas;
This we openly admit.
We have not come to the conclusion
That the virtues of abandonment and realization effortlessly exist
    in us;[38]
This we openly admit.

Myself and all beings, in one voice, admit with heartfelt regret
All these weakened and broken vows, faults,

Bad karma, wrongdoings, and obscurations.
From now on we shall desist from them.

When the marks of mental constructs have totally subsided,
And no thought whatsoever is formed,
What faults are there to admit?
Still, accept this illusory admission from the relative level,
In the state free of reference points,
And cleanse our faults in the space of nonduality.
Please bless us so that our present and future obscurations
May be purified.

Conclusion

The conclusion has five parts.

1. Exhorting and Warding Off

HŪṂ
O lords, who are the display of wisdom,
We exhort your powerful mind to emerge from space and act.
With your buddha activity, annihilate the delusion of
    ego-clinging,
Which is itself the enemy and perpetual troublemaker.

Ward off all present adversities and disharmony,
Bad karma and wrongdoings.
Ward off all harmful tendencies to hold things as real
And to cling to the worldly goals of this life.

And return to primordial purity and great bliss
All "good" and "bad" veils of the moving mind,
Which emerge from the basic nature,
The self-existing uncontrived awareness-wisdom.

2. Receiving the Siddhis

O undeceiving refuges, bless us with your precious wheels
Of imperishable body, speech, mind, qualities, and activity.
Please fulfill these wishes exactly as we have asked
And grant us the ordinary and supreme siddhis.

3. Requesting Forgiveness, Asking the Wisdom Deities to Leave, Dissolving the Mandala

Please forgive any mistake we may have made in this practice.

This self-existing, ultimate deity is unborn, unabiding, and
  unceasing,
Therefore, who is there to summon or ask to leave?

We will dissolve this clear state of empty appearance
Into the innate essence, the natural condition free of limitations.

4. Distribution of Merit and Aspiration

In the state of the threefold purity,[39] we distribute to all beings
All the merit of the three times within samsara and nirvana.
May we enjoy the glory of complete well-being
And quickly attain the unsurpassable vajra state.

5. Auspicious Wishes

May the blazing splendor of auspiciousness saturate samsara and
  nirvana,
Replete with wishes, wholesomeness, and bliss.
All the refuges, the primordial protectors, are the perfect
  dharmadhatu;
May its vast auspiciousness be present.

This completes the practice requested by Lama Karma Dedrol, a very learned Sanskrit scholar. He lived in retreat for three years and recited one hundred million of the six-syllable mantra (OṂ MAṆI PADME HŪṂ). Offering this unsurpassable mandala he asked me to write a practice that included making offerings, fulfilling wishes, admitting faults, asking for protection, and whatever else is needed, directed to all those worthy of veneration without sectarian distinctions. He indicated it should have ultimate teachings of true meaning interwoven with those of the secret path, without clouding them with poetic embellishments.

It was composed by this lazy person called Ngawang Kunga Tenzin, who although following the lineage of ultimate meaning seems to be completely dedicated to accomplishing the meaningless aims of a wandering mind.

By this merit, may the kind sentient beings, boundless as the sky, enjoy the great glory of altruism and happiness of the temporal and ultimate states.[40]

OPENING THE DOOR TO LIBERATION

A Special Condensed Mind Training

TOGDEN SHAKYA SHRI

Namo guru!

With intense veneration from the three doors, I prostrate to the all-pervading Tenpe Nyima Rinpoche, inseparable from the primordial protector. Please bless me with your permission to write a few words on the way of preserving the natural state of mind.

This consists of (1) the foundations and (2) the main body of the practice.

THE FOUNDATIONS

A. Common Foundations

Train your mind to develop conviction on the difficulty of obtaining the favorable conditions of a human birth, death and impermanence, cause and effect of karma, and the shortcomings of samsara. Meditate on these subjects until your attraction to samsara is reverted.

B. Special Foundations

As generally indicated in the Dzogchen tradition, until you have the results, practice refuge and prostrations, meditation and recitation of the Vajrasattva mantra, offering of mandalas, and guru yoga.

Togden Shakya Shri (1853–1919)

Raised in a Drukpa Kagyu monastery, Togden Shakya Shri received Mahamudra and Dzogchen instructions from some of the greatest masters of his time. He established a rustic meditation community that attracted up to seven hundred disciples who practiced meditation zealously. He is renowned for his high realization and having been able to teach both systems completely.

THE MAIN BODY OF THE PRACTICE

This has three parts: (1) the body posture, (2) the shower of the guru's blessings, and (3) the technique for observing the mind.

A. Body Posture

Adopt the posture of the seven points of Vairochana.

B. Shower of the Guru's Blessings

Instantly visualize yourself as Chemchok in union. On the crown of your head, sitting on a seat of a lotus and moon, is the essence of your root guru manifesting in the form of the glorious Samantabhadra. His body is blue, he wears the attire of the dharmakaya, his hands form the meditation mudra, and he is adorned with the major and minor marks of excellence. Embracing his consort, the white dharmadhatu Samantabhadri, he rests amid shimmering lights of the five rainbow colors. Visualizing him clearly, recite aloud the following supplication from deep in your heart and bones:

Kind guru, lord of refuge in this and future lives,
With intense devotion, I supplicate to you.
Bless me so that I may recognize the face of empty awareness,
     primordial purity,
And perfecting the four visions of *thögal*,
May I realize the rainbow body of light.

Recite this with tears pouring from your eyes, feeling the hairs of your body quivering. At the end of the prayer, recite:

From the white OM in the glorious guru's forehead,
White light rays stream forth like the rings of a chain,
Entering the white bindu in my forehead.
The bindu at once becomes a vivid letter OM.

Every single physical negativity and obscuration of all
 my lives are purified.
Bless me so that I may attain the nirmanakaya that tames beings.

From the red ĀḤ in the glorious guru's throat,
Red light rays stream forth like the rings of a chain,
Entering the red bindu in my throat.
The bindu at once becomes a vivid letter ĀḤ.
Every single verbal negativity and obscuration of all my lives are
 purified.
Bless me so that I may attain the unceasing sambhogakaya.

From the blue HŪṂ in the glorious guru's heart,
Blue light rays stream forth like the rings of a chain,
Entering the blue bindu in my heart.
The bindu at once becomes a vivid letter HŪṂ.
Every single mental negativity and obscuration of all my lives is
 purified.
Bless me so that I may attain the unborn dharmakaya.

From the red HRĪḤ in the glorious guru's navel,
Multicolor light rays stream forth like the rings of a chain,
Entering the red bindu in my navel.
The bindu at once becomes a vivid letter HRĪḤ.
Every single negativity and obscuration of my three doors
 together is purified.
Bless me so that I may attain the svabhavikakaya.

Finally, through fervent devotion and yearning,
The guru in union melts into a sphere of light
And blends inseparably as one in the sphere of awareness,
Unutterable, unthinkable, and inexpressible Samantabhadra, the
 mind's expanse.

ĀḤ

Through this, your guru's mind merges instantly with yours. Then rest still for as long as you can. when there is movement, observe nakedly the essence.

C. The Technique for Observing the Mind

The main body of the practice consists of (1) searching for shamatha based on attributes and (2) preserving shamatha without attributes.

1. Searching for Shamatha Based on Attributes

First, place a small pebble in front of yourself and look at it one-pointedly, and do not allow your eyes or consciousness to wander. If the mind does not stay still but instead becomes dispersed, merge the thoughts with the pebble and observe. After just a short while take a rest. Look in this way, for short yet numerous periods, until the experience of stillness becomes longer than before.

After that, visualize a blue letter HŪṂ in your heart. From it, many HŪṂ letters stream forth without interruption and go around the previous pebble clockwise, until the first HŪṂ stands on top of the pebble. Direct your awareness to it. Then the HŪṂ letters return to the HŪṂ in your heart, dissolving one by one into it. Again, take a rest. Meditate on this until your mind becomes somewhat familiarized.

Then your body turns into a blue letter HŪṂ, which remains in the air just about touching the ground. Then send it gradually through the road toward the mountains beyond. Take a rest, while barely keeping this present in your mind. Then, revert the process as before. Meditate repeating these steps several times.

Then, visualize a HŪṂ in your heart and another HŪṂ in front of yourself. The HŪṂ in your heart emits a HŪṂ that strikes the HŪṂ in front, making it glare with increased radiance. This HŪṂ enters through the opening of the Brahma aperture and dissolves in the HŪM in your heart. Meditate on this until you gain some stability. These practices will be of some use for developing stillness. This completes the shamatha with attributes.

2. Preserving the Shamatha without Attributes

Adopt the body posture and the eye gaze as before. Visualize your guru, whose kindness cannot be repaid, on the crown of your head. Supplicate one-pointedly. After dissolving the guru into yourself, while awareness rests loosely, a somewhat vast openness occurs; that is stillness. From that state, a thought unexpectedly arises; that is movement. That which examines stillness and movement is awareness.

Extend the continuity of this meditation, whereby thoughts will at first increase more and more. As this is the first stillness, by preserving that state without getting fed up, thoughts will gradually subside and stillness will gradually increase. There will come a time when even though there is movement, no great harm will be caused on stillness. This is called the intermediate stillness.

By continuing to preserve the meditation in this way, finally there will come a time when stillness is such that it can last for as long as you wish. At that time, you will experience well-being and clear wakefulness. Even if a few thoughts are produced, they do not harm stillness. Such stillness is called shamatha. To gain stability precisely in that is an extremely important point.

When you are observing the essence of that stillness, thoughts arise vividly clear. Look nakedly at them and they will be released into vast openness. That itself is the arising of vipashyana. By constantly preserving this state, the experiences of bliss and clarity will gradually increase. It is important not to become attached to them and continue looking at the essence.

Once stillness, movement, and awareness—preserved as explained—blend into one, even though there may be movement of thoughts, it becomes empty. I think this is greater one-pointedness. At this time, when you are falling asleep, you may feel you are dropping into a precipice or when dreaming, you may have a frightening dream. These trigger you to rest right on that dream for a long time in a state of vast clear openness. Toward the end, you have just a few moments in which you kind of wake up. This may be the clear light.

At that point, apart from constantly maintaining the shepherd of awareness, a state occurs in which somehow there is nothing else to meditate upon. During sleep, sometimes dots of light appear. These increase gradually and, eventually, the whole room becomes visible, as if it is daytime. I have noticed that the above-mentioned clear light and this one somehow alternate with each other.

Then, fervently supplicate to your guru and preserve the practice. By this, the experiences of bliss and clarity you had before completely vanish. Even stillness is not too intense. You don't judge in terms of "this is it" or "this is not that." You do not grasp at whether you are remaining in the natural state or not, or whether it is empty or not. You even start to wonder about what is happening. During sleep, you feel that outer objects and your body become void, and at that moment you are shocked and wake up all of a sudden. During the daytime, a state occurs in which somehow there is nothing else to do except to barely not wander. The vital point is to continue preserving this all the time.

At times, a thought unexpectedly arises. Shout a strong PHEṬ and look to the essence nakedly. Sometimes, shout a strong PHEṬ, integrate space and awareness, and direct your gaze to the sky. By meditating in this way, a state occurs in which somehow awareness and outer phenomena are not split apart as separate. When you are not distracted, a void-like openness occurs in which you do not fixate materialistically on phenomena of the eight groups as being this or that. When you are distracted this does not happen.

At this point, there are too many moments of distraction and forgetfulness. So, it is vital that you maintain the essence of presence again and again through the shepherd of awareness. At this moment, sometimes during sleep you recognize a dim clear light. Other times there is no clarity and you fall into a vast openness.

Occasionally, through that clarity, yourself and what surrounds you become apparent. Now and then, the dream turns into a state where whatever self-arises is self-liberated in the sphere of awareness.

I would think that these events are the ordinary mind, the wisdom mind of the buddhas, the natural state of sentient beings, or the recognition of the naked vision of the essence kaya.

As explained in the Dzogchen texts, through this you will reach the realization of *trekchö*, the development of thögal, and the subsequent liberation of the body into light.

Whether the first, middle, and last experiences arise, you realize the natural state, or you have obstacles, strayings, and so forth depend exclusively on the devotion to your guru. Due to this also I, this old beggar, supplicated only to my guru. And because of my fervent devotion through my guru's kindness just a little realization was born in my mind. Also, if future generations of practitioners would exert themselves in guru devotion, they will find that the profound vital points of all the teachings are present within it. Therefore, I would advise everybody to cherish the supplications to the guru as most important.

Even though you may have realized the nature of mind, unless you enhance it, the realization will not develop. So, this enhancement is of utmost importance. Since the best enhancement is guru devotion, meditate repeatedly on your guru on the crown of your head and supplicate fervently to him until his mind and your mind integrate. This will definitely enhance your realization.

Then, when any of the five gross poisons arise, without suppressing it, look to its essence nakedly and it will turn into vast openness. That is wisdom. Furthermore, if when you hear unbearable evil words such as false accusations, you are capable of liberating that by looking at its nature. Through this your experience will be greatly enhanced.

When beginners are preserving the nature of mind, they will have a lot of dullness, numbness, drowsiness, and so forth. The following are techniques for solving these problems: If awareness is rampantly distracted, let your body and mind rest loose, squint your eyes and direct your gaze to the border of your seat. If you are drowsy, direct your gaze to the sky and tighten awareness a bit. For dullness, direct your eyes upward. With loose awareness, identify one thought, another thought, and so on as they are born. This is important. By practicing in this way, all these problems will be cleared.

———

My Dharma brother Chöphel requested me repeatedly to write profound instructions that would benefit the mind. I do not have even a fraction of a quality in my mind and it is not suitable for a jaded hypocrite such as myself to write beguiling lies. However, unable to turn him back, after supplicating to my refuge Tenpe Nyima—whose kindness cannot be repaid—I, this old beggar Shakya Shri, wrote this at night by the light of butter lamps.[41]

Milarepa Supplication

Togden Shakya Shri

Namo guru ḍākinībhyaḥ!

Refuge

The guru yoga of the inconceivably kind Shepa Dorje begins with refuge.

Namo! Both myself and all beings throughout space,
Until our own enlightenment is won,
Respectfully turn for refuge to the guru and entourage;
And give rise to the supreme attitude—
Wishing that all beings throughout space will achieve ultimate
 awakening.

Arising as the Deity

The emptiness of my usual grasping at ordinary appearance
Is the unobstructed self-radiance of suchness—the yogini.
Seated upon a lotus and moon seat in the space above her head
Is the ever-kind Shepa Dorje.

Dressed in white robes, he shows the gesture of meditation
As he gazes into space.
His empty yet apparent form is a radiant blue.

Hosts of gurus gather around him as he sits at ease,
The head of oceanic hordes of dakinis.

THE ACTUAL SUPPLICATION

A ho ye!

Essence of the buddhas of the three times,
Source of the sublime Dharma of non-attachment,
And supreme among the liberated sangha,
Kindly Shepa Dorje, embodiment of the Three Jewels, care
    for me!

Embodiment of all refuge-granting gurus,
Essence of all awakened yidam deities,
And supreme amidst the oceanic hordes of dakinis,
Kindly Shepa Dorje, embodiment of the Three Roots, care for me!

Crown ornament of the Kagyu teachings,
You are the lord of the ear-whispered secret path.
Skilled in maturing and liberating the fortunate,
Kindly Shepa Dorje, who guides all beings throughout space,
    care for me!

In this and all future lives, I have no one else in whom to place
    my hope or turn to for refuge.
Please hold me in your compassion and, lordly master, care
    for me!

Bestow the supreme empowerment of your form upon my body
And bless me to accomplish the immutable rainbow body.

May the supreme empowerment of your voice enter my speech
And bless me to accomplish the ceaseless unity of
    sound-emptiness.

Bestow the supreme empowerment of your wisdom upon
   my mind
And bless me to realize the dharmakaya of empty-awareness.

The lordly master dissolves into light that becomes nondual with
   the nature of my awareness,
The self-liberation of the ground within the expanse of the
   dharmakaya.

ĀḤ! This is the supplication of the lowly madman Shakya Shri.

The Eighth Khamtrul Dongyu Nyima (1931–1980)

Khamtrul Dongyu Nyima was not only a learned and realized master but also accomplished in painting, sculpture, dance, and traditional crafts. He left Tibet in 1959 and established the Tashi Jong Tibetan settlement and Khampagar Monastery in Kangra, India, upholding all aspects of the Kham Drukpa Kagyu tradition.

Advice for Mountain Retreat

Nectar for the Mind that Wishes for Liberation

The Eighth Khamtrul Dongyu Nyima

Precious guru, no different from all the buddhas,
The supreme light illuminating the unsurpassable path of
perpetual bliss,
Who has the kindness to reveal it in detail to sentient beings,
Thinking of you I prostrate with faith,
And respectfully place you as an ornament on the crown of my head.

Those who have made contact with their pure past aspirations and virtuous karma have the excellent intelligence to direct their interest far away from the worldly involvements of this life. Remaining in solitude, they wish to accomplish permanent well-being for themselves and other beings. For them, here is a brief explanation of the disciplines required.

This world of samsara is by nature suffering, like a prison or a pit of burning coals. Whether born in the higher or lower realms, one never passes beyond this condition. Perceiving it as such, do not be attached to any worldly happiness or wealth and cultivate a mind that genuinely renounces it. You have obtained the best type of body, one that enables you to strenuously apply yourself to the means of gaining liberation. You have been accepted by an authentic guru and have met the essence of the Buddha's teaching. Reflecting on all this, be happy with your extremely good fortune.

However, one does not know how long this vessel-like body will live. The time of death is completely uncertain and the karmic law of cause and effect is unequivocal. Therefore, it would not be right to continue amassing wrongdoings and die without having accomplished the permanent goal. Do not let the opportunities of this precious human body go to waste. Immediately begin your practice and enter the genuine Buddhadharma. Without interruption, maintain an intelligent state of mind that decides, "I will not neglect the great responsibility of diligence under any circumstance."

Put your unshakable trust in the excellent refuge, the Three Jewels, and in your kind root guru who embodies them all. Think, "Whatever you do, you know best," and in this spirit, accept the guru as the only one in whom you can place your hopes without hesitation. Cultivate an uncontrived, fervent devotion for the guru and cut off the ties of wrong views, doubts, a restless mind with too many ideas, and so forth.

Since beginningless time you have had a continuous series of rebirths in this samsaric state. All beings, not only a limited number of them, have alternately been your parents. Realize that they have been as kind to you as your present parents but are now going the wrong way, confused and deluded, wanting happiness but engaging in activities that bring about the opposite. Contemplate this with intense loving-kindness and wish them happiness. With strong compassion, wish them freedom from suffering. Persistently generate the great undertaking of bodhichitta that includes the thought, "I shall single-handedly establish them at the level of Buddhahood." As much as possible, try to eliminate self-cherishing and detrimental clinging to self-centered considerations. Through the highest intention of benefiting others, become accustomed to giving away what makes you happy and taking others' sufferings upon yourself. If you cannot actually do it, just imagine it. Once you are familiar with this, learn to turn whatever you do into something beneficial for others.

You may have to deal with concrete dangerous enemies or with obstacles, hallucinations, and so on, created by spirits intent on disturbing you or causing trouble. No matter what happens, instead of creating much wrongdoing by getting angry, put on the superior armor of patience. Always expand your mind with love and compassion and try your best to be of help. The more you cling to thoughts of "demons" the more numerous and intense the undesirable situations and harm caused by malevolent beings there will be. Knowing them all to be only manifestations of your own mind's deluded conceptions, leave no more room for doubt about it. Thus, tame your mind over and over again.

Instead of censuring people, making them unhappy by abusing or blaming them with harmful intention, regardless of their high or low status, let yourself be flooded with affection and loving-kindness. On seeing faults in others, do not criticize. Instead, look at your own faults and recognize them. Try your best to discipline this unruly mentality, bad disposition, and habits.

There may be certain small and large virtuous actions that you still cannot perform. When you see them being performed by others, such as your guru, Dharma brothers, other practitioners, or lay devotees, regardless of their position, do not become competitive or envious. Rejoicing in their deeds, do your best by various means to accumulate a great amount of immaculate wholesome actions.

Thinking, "Such a lowly person as I cannot help others," you become frustrated and disheartened. Put aside these feelings and take on yourself the suffering of all beings. No matter what unwanted events you encounter, such as sickness and misfortune, feel joyful, as past karma is thus exhausted. In addition, imagine that you take upon yourself all the pain, wrongdoings, and obscurations of all beings. When this actually does happen, take any adversity as the path to enlightenment by means of such joyous determination.

Never let your mind wander or be without concern for your practice. Always rest naturally in the conviction that the essence of the self-arising mind has been empty from the very beginning. Do not grasp at the natural expressions of the mind, the experiences of bliss and clarity, or the union of these two, but relax at ease. Avoid acceptance and rejection, such as manipulating your meditation by thinking, "This is meditation; I am doing this; this is what

I need." Do not be absorbed by a continuous state of delusion in which you are not recognizing the undercurrent of subtle wandering thoughts. Whatever thoughts of subject or object arise, simply recognize them. Without grasping, relax in that state of awareness. Other than this, forget about the fabricated process of struggling with remedies to eliminate the undesirable, which is suppressing something and pursuing something else.

Once you have recognized the stark, clear awareness that transcends dualistic mind and is absolutely uninfluenced by thoughts of the three times, keep it always present through mindfulness, with or without effort. Thus, go about your daily activities without desire or clinging. The essential teaching, expounded from many points of view in all the sutras, tantras, and profound ways, is none other than the means of seeing the naked, empty awareness, the real face of the ultimate nature. Therefore, exert yourself unremittingly in this.

At the end of your practice session, dedicate all the merit of yourself and others for the attainment of supreme enlightenment for the sake of all beings, just as the buddhas and bodhisattvas of all times have done. Do this in a state where the three spheres—yourself, sentient beings, and the merit to be distributed—are not conceptualized. Then, without just mechanically repeating them, make prayers of aspiration that you may be able to engage in even a fraction of the deeds and liberating lifestyles of the buddhas, their spiritual sons, and all the great saints and teachers of the past. Carry out your practice observing the three instructions[42] concerning preparation, the main body, and conclusion of a practice, in a complete form without allowing it to become sloppy. Through these three points it is very important to make any virtuous action you perform significant, whether corresponding to the accumulations of merit, wisdom, or both in union.

If one has acquired mastery over the unity of appearances and mind, it makes no difference where one remains in retreat. Beginners, however, should stay in a mountain hermitage, in a retreat place endowed with great blessing. It should be congenial and pleasant, where necessities are easily available. It should be isolated from the hustle and bustle of the world, and devoid of bad companions, such as vicious people and persons with wrong views. Your dwelling, friends, household things, and possessions should be sufficient, however simple they may be. There is no need for further paraphernalia—you should possess the wealth of contentment.

Do not associate with bad companions who pretend to be religious but are accustomed to behaving without Dharma and have an immoral outlook. Do not rely on a teacher who teaches wrong views and behavior. Whether you enter the right path or not depends on whether your guru is properly qualified. Therefore, search for the right spiritual friend. Having examined him, serve him well through the three ways of pleasing a teacher.[43] Avoid embroiling your own mind with masses of discursive, insubstantial words, or piling up ideas or things. Do not be satisfied with taking a little bit of vital instruction—of teaching, which is the quintessence of his enlightened mind—and leaving it at that. Request from your guru the whole of the teaching without leaving anything out.

Scrutinize it earnestly and resolve correctly any misunderstandings regarding the doubtful points. Through the strength of your meditative experience deepen your conviction. Successively integrate in your being the learning, reflection, and meditation of the complete instructions, including those on avoiding pitfalls and enhancing the practice. Thus, make sure you are entering the unerring path.

It is a great loss to take bits and pieces of all kinds of teachings renowned to be very profound, having mere intellectual understanding of them and leaving it at that, without gaining confidence or first-hand experience in any of them. Once the instructions have merged with your being, you will see that the central topics of all Dharma teachings—whether imparted directly, indirectly, or by their own strength—have been taught with a common criterion and purpose. Thus, the different paths or their outcomes are all compatible. The teachings you were given by your root guru are in accordance with your own faculties and particular fortune.

Consider them all-sufficient, merge them all into one point and put them into practice. They will then be most effective.

Do not evaluate or criticize the diverse Buddhist traditions and different schools of thought, or the teachers holding those lineages who appear to be of either important or humble position—whoever they may be. The skillful deeds that buddhas and bodhisattvas display in all kinds of illusory ways in accordance with the inclinations and capacities of those who are to be trained cannot be weighed by the minds of ordinary people. To see them as good or bad is a sign that one's mind is biased. Do not find fault with them, for if there is no faith the seed of Dharma becomes rotten from its core. Regard your perception as being perverted by your impure, deluded conceptions and adhere to this understanding. Be conscientious about it and discipline your faith and pure perception so that it becomes impartial.

When meditating on a deity, reciting mantra, and the like, follow the corresponding authoritative texts and be determined to perform them precisely as explained there. Do not do your practice casually, the easy way. Once you have taken the commitment to do that practice in retreat do not allow yourself to be diverted by any other circumstance whatsoever. If it is difficult for the attributes of realization to be born in your being, or if the signs that indicate you are close to accomplishing the deity take a long time to appear, do not become impatient or frustrated or develop wrong views and doubts. Stand firm in your devotion, including the three kinds of faith—admiration, aspiration, and trust.

Make a strong commitment to generate unflinching resolve and constantly maintain it with perfect diligence. Supplicate with great devotion to your guru and yidam, who are inseparable, and take the empowerments. Admit your weakened and broken samaya, wrongdoings, downfalls, and whatever has conflicted with the Dharma and endeavor to keep your vows thereafter. Accumulate merit by making large amounts of actual or visualized offerings according to the practice. Without clinging to a self, take all good and bad situations as the path, especially so when you have a lot of happiness and wealth and an abundance of property, friends, and possessions. Feeling satisfied and delighted with these opens the door through which many subtle, obstructing spirits sneak through unnoticed. These will steadily cause a natural postponement of your Dharma practice. You should be able to recognize them and use them as the path.

Aiming at wealth with the basis of apparently doing altruistic work for others is wrong livelihood, and by doing so there is a great danger of cutting the life vein of your own liberation. Try your best to abstain from this and strengthen your actions by profound distribution of merit and pure aspiration. Do not allow yourself to merely become a Dharma practitioner like one at the end of these decadent times who is hollow like a taxidermist's dummy. Instead, take as an example the liberating lifestyles of past siddhas and remain in solitude in the mountains. Always check and examine within and see whether your mind is caught in the grip of attachment to the eight worldly preoccupations[44] involving desire or aversion, hope or fear, and the like. Enthusiastically take up the hardships connected with Dharma practice. Be capable of ignoring your own suffering. Avoid doing things that will make you ashamed of yourself. Be someone who is confident of dying without regrets. Follow in the footsteps of the enlightened beings of the past.

Although you may have gained the signs of progress in your experience and realization, do not cling to these as being something good, and avoid becoming conceited. Even though you may have some good qualities, do not spread the word around. However high your level of confidence regarding the view and meditation, do not overlook the relative plane of the phenomenal world. Outwardly carrying out all your activities with purity, you should be worthy of being a beautiful ornament of the Dharma. It may already be appropriate for you to practice the outrageous tantric actions.[45] However, you should be skillful at it, for it would not be right if your behavior caused the unruly beings of these decadent times—who regard the Dharma and people in a distorted way—to stray toward the abyss of the miserable realms. Do not be governed by likes and dislikes or attachment and aversion toward the people you know, whether you have a good or bad rapport with them. Instead, take hold of all those connected to you by making pure wishes to become of benefit to them.

In brief, emphasis is put on the following points which subsume all the preceding instructions: Feel immeasurable joy, faith, and longing, having met the profound path of the unsurpassable mystery that leads to the primordial land of liberation in one lifetime. Do not let the teachings you have received from the mouth of your holy guru remain at the stage of having merely requested and heard them. Avoid being caught up by doubts and hesitation. Merging together devotion and diligence, make full use of the opportunities provided by your precious human existence. Make your own mind your judge. Do not offend the buddhas of the three times.

Because, in such a deluded person as I, there is neither understanding of the numerous teachings I have heard nor any real confidence, experience nor realization has sprung from reflection and meditation. These instructions and words of advice are like a blind man leading others. In addition to not having any special value for clarifying your practice, indeed, this advice will only cause people to criticize me and me to become ashamed of myself. Believing clay to be gold, you have persistently asked me to write this as you specified, which I have done only not to turn my back on your request. But as this work lacks the quintessence of the vital instructions, I beg you to not rely on this alone and kindly bring to your attention the numerous teachings on mountain retreat written by the great saints. In particular, please consult *Extracting the Quintessence of Accomplishment*,[46] a concise, easy-to-understand text, full of the pith of profound teachings written by Jigdral Yeshe Dorje, Dudjom Rinpoche.

This instruction on mountain retreat called "The Nectar of the Mind Wishing for Liberation" was requested by the yogin Lama Yeshe Rabsel, who offered me a scarf and three coins of silver some time ago. It was written by me, Kalzang Dongyu Nyima, who comes from southern Kham, a hollow man of the termination of these decadent times in the form of a monk, dull and insignificant, who walks at the end of the line of followers of the lineage of real meaning. I composed it in the Iron Ox Year, 1961, on the eighteenth day of the first month at Kalimpong, in the Aryan country of India, at the top of the mountain Durping, in my house called Chime Deden Photrang, the Blissful Palace of Immortality, close to the monastery Zangdog Palri, the Glorious Copper-Colored Mountain. May it cause goodness to become supreme.[47]

Trulshik Adeu Rinpoche (1931–2007)

The Eighth Adeu Rinpoche was educated in Tsechu Monastery in Nangchen, Tibet. Later, while in prison, he received many Nyingma teachings from Khenpo Munsel and other masters. He later rebuilt Tsechu Monastery and passed on the Khampa Drukpa lineage to large numbers of tulkus, lamas, and monks both inside and outside of Tibet.

SONG OF GROUND, PATH, AND FRUITION

ADEU RINPOCHE

Ordinary mind is uncontrived, the innate natural state;
Its nature is empty, lucid, and unimpeded.
The common basis of samsara and nirvana,
Unsullied by fabrication, as it is, the natural state of the ground.

It is realized by insight that fully distinguishes phenomena
As the equality of emptiness and compassion,
Awareness and basic space.
So, as for that, do not recall, do not imagine, do not examine,
Do not meditate, and do not intellectualize.
The natural flow is the essence itself.
Through undistracted mindfulness
The nature will be completely known.
Sustaining the continuity, beyond conceptual designations,
Is the principal path.

Whatever arises is self-liberated,
Naturally present great wisdom.
Profound and luminous co-emergence
Is endowed with all supreme aspects.
All that appears and exists
Naturally arises as the three kayas,
Beyond partiality.
The indivisibility of composure and post-meditation,
Is the mahamudra of fruition.

To fulfill the wishes of Khenpo Yeshe Gyaltsen, who possesses the supreme qualities of the three trainings, this was offered as it popped up in the mind by the one named Druprik Khyuchok, who is a mere intellectual, devoid of experience.

May it be virtuous!

NOTES

1. From the *Mahamudratilaka:* | *nges tshig ni* | | *phyag ni stong pa'i ye shes te* | | *rgya ni 'khor ba'i chos las grol* | | *chen po zung 'jug rtogs pa yin* | |.
2. Daniel P. Brown explores this issue in *Pointing out the Great Way* (Somerville, MA:Wisdom, 2006)..
3. Ulrigh Iimme Kragh addresses this further in "Culture and Subculture— A Study of the Mahāmudrā Teachings of Sgam po pa" (master's thesis, University of Copenhagen, 1998).
4. The translator wishes to thank Chögyam Trungpa Rinpoche and the Nalanda Translation Committee, Karl Brunnhölzl, and Ari Kiev for their beautiful translations of this same text, which were consulted for clarification and inspiration.
5. Translated by Gerardo Abboud with valuable editing suggestions by Nona Olivia.
6. The meaning of this is explained by Khunu Rinpoche: "Through one-pointed mind, you will realize mahamudra."
7. In this quotation from the *bShes sbrin* (*Suhrllekha*), Nagarjuna is addressing King Sukhacharya (*bDe spyod*). Focusing mindfulness on the body means to observe the body at all times: while standing, sitting, and so forth.
8. The full quotation is: "Mindfulness is not to forget something one is acquainted with; it is the fortunate condition of not wandering at all."
9. A traditional four-line prayer of refuge in the Drukpa Kagyu lineage: "Together with all beings, my mothers, numbering as vast as space, I take refuge in the Guru, the Buddha, and the dharmakaya / . . . the sambhogakaya / . . . the compassionate nirmanakaya / . . . the precious Buddha."
10. "The main purpose of counting the breath (inhaling, holding, and exhaling count as one) is to find stillness of mind. A subsidiary result is that one comes to know with certainty the number of times one breathes in a whole day." From Yongdzin Jampal Pawo's *Commentary on Mahamudra*. See Tsadra Foundation's Rigpe Dorje Practice Series, *Book 11*, 2010.

11. "Investigating, one understands that the movement of the breath neither occurs from the entire body nor from a part of it, and comes to know that the characteristic of the breath is that it arises from a coincidence of factors (*tendrel*)." From Yongdzin Jampal Pawo's *Commentary on Mahamudra.*

12. "As subsidiary result, one sees and captures the colors of the five pranas: earth-prana (yellow), water-prana (white), fire-prana (red), air-prana (black), and space-prana (blue). One also captures their lengths: starting from a distance of sixteen finger-widths in front of one's nose towards oneself is the space-prana; from the fifteenth is the air-prana; from the fourteenth is the fire-prana; from the thirteenth is the water-prana; and from the twelfth is the earth-prana. As these are exhaled, they gradually decrease their one finger-width length, and as they enter into the body they gradually increase it." From Yongdzin Jampal Pawo's *Commentary on Mahamudra.*

13. "By examining each of the five element-pranas distinctly, one captures their movement, lengths, colors and so forth. On account of this, one comes to know how the strength and frequency of the in-out movement of the breath gradually decrease." From Khewang Sangye Dorje's *Commentary on "Notes on Mahamudra."*

14. "When the breath goes out from the nose, visualize that it is expelled as a series of white OM letters resounding like OM. When it comes in, imagine it turns into a series of blue HUM letters resounding like HUM. While it stays, feel that it has turned into one or many red ĀH letters resounding like ĀH remaining below the navel. In this way, turning the exhalation, inhalation and abiding of the breath into the three letters, pay attention to its dispersion, concentration and stillness . . . The fruition of this practice is that the breath ceases to move. Since the breath does not move externally, the mind that is supported by it does not wander to objects and thus subsequent mental occurrences cease." Yongdzin Jampal Pawo's *Commentary on Mahamudra.*

15. According to the oral instructions of some lamas of the lineage, "alternation" in this case means to supersede the first method with the second one. According to Khunu Rinpoche, one should alternate back and forth between both methods until a balance between tightness and looseness is found.

16. *Dran shes.* This term combines mindfulness (*dran pa*) and knowing (*shes bzhin*). In his commentary to this text, Khewang Sangye Dorje defines them by quoting Pema Karpo:

The ability to remain resting for whatever length of time
Is essentially mindfulness.
Mindfulness is the name for nondistraction.
Within nondistraction, thought movement is cognized.
That cognitive aspect is knowing.

He then adds, "The decision, 'I will not be distracted,' made at the outset
is mindfulness. However, considering that it is a preceding factor, it is
called 'determination' (*'dun pa*). The main body, nondistraction or non-
forgetfulness, is called 'mindfulness.' The cognition of stillness and movement springing from that state of mindfulness is known as 'knowing.' . . .
Since these two (*dran pa* and *shes bzhin*) occur at the same time, they are
coupled into the one term, mindful knowing (*dran shes*). . . . Since 'right
thinking' (*tshul bzhin yid la byed pa*) is by nature both mindfulness and
knowing, considering nondistraction they are one, and in terms of their
function they are two. In any case they do not conflict."

17. "It is the view that asserts nothing because it transcends expression,
    thought, knowledge and description." From Khewang Sangye Dorje's
    Commentary.

18. "By examining through discernment stillness and movement, the knowl-
    edge (*prajna*) that understands egolessness arises all of a sudden. This, in
    turn, cleanses stillness and movement (revealing them) as having no true
    nature, after which that knowledge itself also becomes nonconceptual.
    This is similar to what happens with the fire that burns the two pieces of
    wood, which itself becomes extinguished after the wood totally burns
    out." From Khewang Sangye Dorje's *Commentary*.

19. Reverse meditation is an approach where one tackles that which is to
    be abandoned in an opposite way. For example, in the practice of chöd,
    instead of asking for protection from attacks by harmful spirits one
    invites them and offers one's body.

20. *Ngag gi dbang po* is a common epithet of Manjushri, but also could refer
    to Pema Karpo's teacher Ngawang Chokyi Gyalpo.

21. In *Notes on Mahamudra* (*Phyag chen zin bris*, 7a), Pema Karpo defines
    this more: "the knower of stillness and occurrence at this time is correct
    mental engagement (*tshul bzhin yid la byed pa*) or discriminating wis-
    dom (*so sor rtog pa'i shes rab*) and self-awareness (*rang rig pa*)."

22. Chapter 5, vv. 40–41. Translation from the Padmakara Translation
    Group, *The Way of the Bodhisattva* (Boston: Shambhala, 1999), 67–68.

23. "Summit of worldly existence" describes the highest of the mundane
    formless meditations (*arupya-samapatti*).

24. Saraha, *Doha Kosha*, 57.
25. *Bodhicharyavatara*, chapter 9, vv. 32–34.
26. The space of unity is the mental space wherein phenomena are perceived as empty of substantial nature, i.e., phenomena and emptiness arise in union.
27. Mind-made limitations are fabricated (*spros pa*) extreme (*mtha'*) views the mind can fall into. They are all contained in the four extremes of existence, nonexistence, both existent and nonexistent, and neither existent nor nonexistent.
28. Visualization is the development stage (*bskyed rim*). The meditative state is the completion stage (*rdzogs rim*). These two stages are to be practiced in union.
29. The treasures of a chakravartin, or ruler of world systems, include the precious wheel, jewel, queen, minister, elephant, horse, and general.
30. The precious parasol, golden fish, vase, lotus, white conch shell, knot of eternity, victory banner, and golden wheel.
31. The mirror, vermillion dye, white conch shell, *giwang* medicine, *durva* grass, *bilva* fruit, curd, and white mustard seed.
32. Fabulous wealth such as the jeweled mountain of the eastern continent, the uncultivated harvests of the northern continent, etc.
33. The single dot (*thig le nyag gcig*) is the sphere of the dharmakaya, or the instantaneous awareness (*skad gcig ma'i rig pa*), which embraces samsara and nirvana. Since it pervades everything, its play is unobstructed, or transparent (*zang thal*).
34. Teachings of true meaning are those belonging to the path of liberation (*sgrol lam*), such as Mahamudra. The secret path is the path of means (*thabs lam*), which includes, among other practices, the six yogas of Naropa.
35. When resting in equanimity (*mnyam gzhag*) there are no concepts whatsoever. In order to enhance the practice, after arising from that state the meditator checks back (*rjes shes*; literally: "ensuing knowledge or perception") on it, recollecting the various factors that indicate its quality, such as clarity. Once a practitioner of Mahamudra has arrived at the yoga of nonmeditation, his meditation and post-meditation (*mnyam gzhag* and *rjes thob*) have merged into one. Whatever arises then is spontaneous (*rang shar*) because it is the expression of his natural mind and is thus self-liberated (*rang grol*). If, however, he continues to check back at this stage, this is a defect of practice and is therefore admitted as a fault. This explanation of the terms is according to this particular context, and may be explained elsewhere in different ways.

36. All phenomena and experiences being natural expressions of emptiness, there is no reason whatsoever to prefer one as opposed to another. Yet one prefers good experiences to bad ones, stillness to thought movement, and so forth. Moreover, instead of perceiving phenomena with a completely open mind, one might adhere to one point of view, e.g., Mahamudra, while the actual Mahamudra view is the non-view. This would be like looking at the sky through a window instead of out in the open.

37. The conditions for the accomplishment of the *rupakayas* (sambhogakaya and nirmanakaya) are established by accumulating merit.

38. Abandonment comprises all we need to purify and realization comprises all that is to be realized. After completing the path, the virtues, or qualities, these become totally developed and we realize that they had always existed inherently in our basic nature.

39. Threefold purity is to not conceptualize the three spheres (offeror, offering, and recipient of the offering).

40. Translated by Gerardo Abboud and edited by Jon Weinberger and Daniel Staffler, according to the explanations of Drugu Chögyal Rinpoche and Venerable Gegen Khyentse Gyamtso.

41. Translated by Gerardo Abboud with the kind assistance of Venerable Chögyal Rinpoche.

42. The three instructions: (a) Preparation: to set one's motivation toward Buddhahood for the sake of all beings; (b) Main body: to carry out one's practice mindfully without distraction, and in a nonconceptual state if one has such realization; and (c) Conclusion: to distribute the merit to all beings for the attainment of enlightenment.

43. The three ways of pleasing a teacher are to offer him material objects, to serve him, and to practice.

44. The eight worldly preoccupations: pleasure, pain, gain, loss, praise, blame, fame, and disgrace.

45. Outrageous tantric actions involve some actions practiced by tantric practitioners that are not in accordance with what is conventionally accepted as proper. Many examples can be found in the life stories of "mad" yogins such as Drukpa Kunleg and others.

46. This teaching has been translated and published in: H.H. Dudjom Rinpoche, *Extracting the Quintessence of Accomplishment* (Corralitos, CA: Vajrayana Foundation, 1998).

47. Translated by Gerardo Abboud and edited by Ward Brisick, under the kind guidance of the Venerable Chögyal Rinpoche and the Venerable Gegen Khyentse Gyamtso.

Drukpa Kagyu yogis from Tashi Jong